Self-Employment:

From Dream to Reality!

An Interactive Workbook
for Starting Your Small Business

Third Edition

By Linda D. Gilkerson and Theresia M. Paauwe

jist Works
America's Career Publisher®

Self-Employment: From Dream to Reality!, Third Edition

An Interactive Workbook for Starting Your Small Business

© 2008 by Linda D. Gilkerson and Theresia M. Paauwe

Published by JIST Works, an imprint of JIST Publishing
7321 Shadeland Station, Suite 200
Indianapolis, Indiana 46256-3923
Phone: 800-648-JIST   Fax: 877-454-7839
E-mail: info@jist.com   Web site: www.jist.com

Note to instructors. Support materials are available for *Self-Employment: From Dream to Reality!,* Third Edition. An instructor's resources CD-ROM, published by JIST Works, contains helpful guidance and many activities and assignments that can be used for adults. Call 800-648-JIST or visit www.jist.com for details. Coauthor Theresia Paauwe is available to "train the trainer." Visit her Web site at www.BusinessMattersTR.com for details.

About career materials published by JIST. Our materials encourage people to be self-directed and to take control of their destinies. We work hard to provide excellent content, solid advice, and techniques that get results. If you have questions about this book or other JIST products, call 800-648-JIST or visit www.jist.com.

Quantity discounts are available for JIST products. Have future editions of JIST books automatically delivered to you on publication through our convenient standing order program. Please call 800-648-JIST or visit www.jist.com for a free catalog and more information.

Visit www.jist.com. Find out about our products, get free tables of contents and sample pages, order a catalog, and link to other career-related sites. You can also learn more about JIST authors and JIST training available to professionals.

Acquisitions Editor: Susan Pines
Development Editor: Dave Anderson
Cover and Interior Designer: Aleata Halbig
Proofreader: Jeanne Clark
Indexer: Kelly D. Henthorne

Printed in the United States of America

12 11 10 09 08 07   9 8 7 6 5 4 3 2 1

ISBN 978-1-59357-520-5

Just What You Need to Get Started

Self-Employment: From Dream to Reality!, Third Edition, is unlike any other book about starting your own business. What makes it so unique?

- It is an interactive workbook full of helpful worksheets and exercises that get you involved in decision-making and show you examples of many aspects of running your business.

- It is based on the authors' proven self-employment training course and on their experiences as small business operators. You learn small-business basics through a tried-and-true approach used by thousands of other would-be entrepreneurs.

- It is just right for first-time entrepreneurs. You learn what it takes to succeed in easy-to-understand language and without getting bogged down in hundreds of pages of detail.

You can turn your dream into reality. Let this workbook show you how.

Table of Contents

Introduction

In the early 1990s, Linda Gilkerson and I met while working for a microenterprise program helping aspiring and existing entrepreneurs realize their dream of being self-employed. Having both been self-employed, we shared a passion for fostering entrepreneurship. Together, we provided classroom training and technical assistance to hundreds of entrepreneurs, and before long, this book was born.

Today, microenterprise programs, schools, community-based organizations, and entrepreneurship programs throughout the United States use this workbook to help dreamers conceive and write business plans.

This workbook is designed to guide you through the process of launching a business by introducing key business concepts in practical, simple-to-understand ways. Worksheets and exercises are designed to encourage a hands-on approach to learning. By completing the exercises in each chapter, you collect all the information you need to put together a business plan one step at a time.

Linda and I are extremely pleased that nearly ten years after its initial publication, *Self-Employment: From Dream to Reality!* is now available in its third edition. We see this as proof that the dream of being self-employed remains alive and well and that the reality is indeed attainable. If anything, the path to self-employment is even easier and more well traveled now than it was a decade ago, a trend that is reflected in the new and revised material in this book. Some of the changes in this edition include information about the U.S. Small Business Administration loan guarantee program; some popular pricing strategies and an alternative method for determining breakeven; a simplified system for managing small business paperwork; a more detailed plan for creating goals and action steps; and a new bonus chapter on e-commerce.

Whether self-employment is something you'd like to learn more about, a dream you've been pursuing, or how you make a living, you will find valuable information in this book. We'd love to hear from you, so please, consider sharing your comments, questions, and stories with us at the e-mail address below. Good luck on your journey of turning your self-employment dream into a reality!

Theresia M. Paauwe, President
Business Matters Training Resources, Inc.
TP@BusinessMattersTR.com

CHAPTER 1

The World of Business

Owning a business has always been part of the American dream, but today more people than ever are considering self-employment. Maybe you're thinking of starting a business because you've been "downsized." Perhaps you have the technology to work from home. Or maybe you just looked at the quality of your life and decided you need a change.

In this chapter, we look at the reasons people give for going into business for themselves. We explore the personality traits of successful business owners. We review the main reasons that businesses fail and look at how to avoid many of these pitfalls. And we show you why *planning* your business is not only time well spent but the only way to create a healthy and profitable venture.

In the space below, list all your answers to this question: *Why do you want to own a business?*

_____

_____

_____

_____

Of course, there are no right or wrong answers to this question. But your reasons are important because they will be the measure of your success. For instance, say one of the reasons you list is spending more time with your children. If, a year after starting your business, you find you are working more hours than ever before and actually seeing your children less, is your business a success? Or perhaps you want to own a business to make more money. If, after several years, you are still stretching to pay your bills, is your business a success?

One of the best things about self-employment is that you get to define what success means. And your definition is shaped by the reasons you want to go into business.

Before we go any further, we want to define two terms we use throughout this book:

- **Entrepreneur:** One who manages, organizes, and assumes the risk of a business or enterprise.
- **Microenterprise:** A very small business that operates from a home, storefront, or office and employs five or fewer employees (and often only one!).

Do You Have What It Takes?

Successful entrepreneurs come from all sorts of backgrounds and experiences. Age, gender, marital status, and education levels do not seem to be significant factors for success. But successful entrepreneurs share certain skills. As you look through the following checklist, determine the areas in which you excel and identify the areas in which you need work.

- ❑ Are you responsible? Do you do what you say you will do when you say you will do it? Can people count on you? Entrepreneurs accept responsibility for their own businesses.
- ❑ Do you have good social skills? Do you say what you mean? Do you listen well? Entrepreneurs must be able to sell themselves.
- ❑ Are your financial and personal situations stable? Entrepreneurs need to be in good shape financially and emotionally to be able to concentrate on their new business.
- ❑ Are you optimistic? Entrepreneurs think positively.
- ❑ Do you have a strong motivation to achieve? Entrepreneurs are doers.
- ❑ Are you a hard worker? Do you work hard for others? Entrepreneurs often work more than 40 hours per week.
- ❑ Do you have problem-solving skills? Entrepreneurs are proficient problem solvers.
- ❑ Are you independent? Entrepreneurs are leaders, not followers.
- ❑ Are you afraid of making decisions? Entrepreneurs have a take-charge attitude.

Following is a list of personality traits that are common to successful entrepreneurs. How many of them do you possess?

- ❑ Motivation to achieve
- ❑ Capacity for continued hard work
- ❑ Nonconformity
- ❑ Strong leadership ability
- ❑ Street smarts
- ❑ Responsibility
- ❑ Optimistic outlook

Some personality traits are *not* conducive to successful entrepreneurship, including these:

- ❑ Compulsive in gambling
- ❑ High risk taking
- ❑ Impulsive or inclined to "shoot from the hip"

Finally, successful entrepreneurs have skills to sell. What skills and experiences do you have that are key to the success of the business you want to own?

_____

_____

_____

_____

Business Failure

We've all heard the bad news. Here are some common statistics that scare many people away from self-employment:

- One in three new businesses fail within six months.
- Three out of four start-ups shut down within five years.
- Nine out of ten companies operating today will eventually fail.

Scary statistics indeed. But before you become discouraged, consider the fact that these figures do not tell the whole story. Many of the "failures" are more accurately called "career changes," as no money was lost and the closure of the company was voluntary. In fact, many owners of the closed businesses considered their businesses successful but decided to cease operation for many reasons: The hours were too long, the market changed, or the owners could make more money by working for someone else.

So, although some businesses do fail, the chances for success are better than you might think.

Why Do Businesses Fail?

Why do you think businesses fail? _____

_____

_____

Compare your answers to some of these reasons for business failure. Knowing some of the pitfalls *before* you start your business can help you avoid them. We address most of these problems in this workbook.

- **Owner's personality not suited to running a business.** Business owners who are reluctant to make decisions or who lack self-discipline have a greater chance of failing. Businesses run on relationships. Customers need to trust the owner so they will be comfortable doing business with him or her. A business owner who has difficulty getting along with people will be at a disadvantage.

- **Poor choice of business opportunity.** Some fields in the marketplace are saturated. For example, it seems you can't drive a city block without seeing a pizza place, a coffee shop, or a video store. Having lots of competition means that you must have something terrific to offer customers that your competitors don't. These are risky business ventures, simply because there are so many of them.

- **Inadequate start-up capital.** Many businesses begin without enough money in reserve. Chances are, finding customers and generating enough income to support the business will take longer than you expect. On the other hand, if you make good decisions when spending your start-up capital, you may actually need less money than you originally estimate.

  In the beginning, invest your cash in people and things that will result in sales—not in "flash." Forget the fancy office and the latest gadgets *unless they are absolutely necessary for you to make sales.* Sometimes leasing or renting equipment can save you money during the start-up phase. Ask yourself this question before you buy anything: How will this expenditure result in sales?

- **Poor selection of location.** If you are locating your business outside your home, choose your spot based on where your customers live, shop, or visit. Do not base this decision on proximity to your home. Don't take a space simply because it happens to be available on the first day you're looking. Try to leave your emotions out of the decision. This is especially important for retail businesses. When you're looking at a potential spot, ask yourself this question: Will your customers come to this location to purchase your products or services?

- **Lack of knowledge about attracting customers.** You must have a plan to get customers to try your product or service. You can't simply offer lower prices than your competitors and be successful. Remember, consumers are creatures of habit. They must have a reason to change their spending habits.

- **Failure to seek professional advice.** It is critical that you seek the advice of an accountant and, depending on your business, an attorney. Save yourself grief by finding and hiring an accountant in the beginning. Your business may also require other professionals. You probably have expertise in the business you have chosen, but you are probably not an authority on every aspect of your business.

- **Poor choice of legal form.** You need to understand the different legal forms of business so you can make an informed decision about which is best for you. We discuss sole proprietorships, partnerships, and different types of corporations in Chapter 8. There are many factors to consider, and taxes are an important one. So this may be a decision you want to discuss with your accountant and attorney.

- **Insufficient experience in product or service.** Some people dive into a business without understanding how that particular industry works. As a result, they may set up a pricing structure that will not allow them to make a profit. Or they might produce an inferior product or service. Successful business owners either have experience in the industry or take the time to research it thoroughly *before* taking the plunge.

- **Insufficient planning and investigation.** Some people spend more time planning their vacations than they do planning their careers. Surprises will always happen, but if you take the time to plan, fewer issues are left to chance. Planning will accomplish one of two things: (1) You will decide that your business idea won't work or that you are not ready; or (2) you will be convinced that you have a good idea that can work, and you will be comfortable with the risk of self-employment.

> *Remember, a business owner who fails to plan plans to fail!*

What is your biggest challenge for business ownership? How will you overcome it?

_____

_____

_____

_____

Planning Your Business Is Critical

Many people float aimlessly through life, taking its ups and downs as they come, just getting by and living from day to day. If they become successful, or even comfortable, it's more by accident than by plan. This approach rarely works for a business.

Proper planning allows you to try out your business on paper with no financial risk. Your plan is your road map: It tells you where you should be at any given time, when you are succeeding, when you need to make adjustments, even when it's time to get out.

It's impossible to know everything you need to before going into business. The sheer amount of information is staggering. But you should figure out what you need to know before starting the business and then plan to continue learning.

> ***Learn to plan and plan to learn!***

Your Best Bet Is a Business Plan

If you have spent any time researching self-employment, you probably have encountered the concept of a *business plan*. And if you are like most people, the more you read about business plans, the more confused you became. There are several different outlines to choose from, all with different sections. Some outlines use questions, some use big business jargon. The usual conclusion people come to is that business plans are very complicated. But they don't have to be. A business plan can be a simple, effective tool for planning, financing, and growing your business.

Before we discuss what a business plan should look like, take a look at why a business plan is critical to your success:

- **A business plan can give you the confidence to start your business, or it can help you realize that your business idea is not a good one.** Before you make the final decision, you need to think through the answers to many questions about your product or service, your customers, your pricing, your marketing, and your potential cash flow. Your business plan gives you a process for answering those questions in an organized and logical way.

- **After you start your business, you can refer back to your business plan to keep you focused on the next task.** A business plan is never finished. It changes as circumstances in your business change. You can use it as a guide to build and manage a successful business.

- **A business plan is a small business's best tool for raising money.** Most financial institutions will insist on a business plan to evaluate your idea. Your business plan gives the loan officer information about you and your idea and allows him or her to evaluate your business's creditworthiness.

- **A business plan can be a marketing tool.** As you write your business plan, you will have a clearer picture of your business. This will help you explain what services or products your business will provide, who your customers will be, and what your goals are for the business. Have your employees read your business plan so they understand what you want to accomplish.

The Contents of a Business Plan

You will find an outline of a business plan on the following pages. As you read it, don't get hung up on the information you don't have. This workbook leads you through the steps of gathering information for your own business plan, and we include a sample business plan in Appendix A.

Business Plan Outline

1. Introduction

Title page

Name of business and your name.

Your address and telephone number.

Write the words "Business Plan" on the title page.

Table of contents

Pages should be numbered.

General description of the business

Describe the business you want to start.

What services or products will you offer?

Where will you locate?

Explain why you chose this business.

What are the skills and experiences you bring to the business?

What are your goals for the business?

What is your action plan to achieve these goals?

2. Marketing

Product or service description

What is your product/service?

What is the demand for your product/service?

Market description

Who is your customer?

How do you know?

Describe any market research by industry experts or any research you have done.

How will your market grow or change over the next few years?

Competition

List your competitors and identify their strengths and weaknesses.

Compare prices, product quality, etc.

What advantages will your business have over the competition?

Selling strategy

How will you sell your product or service?

What is your pricing strategy?

What advertising will you do?

What promotions will you do?

How will your product or service be delivered?

3. Organization

Quality control

How will you ensure the quality of your products or services?

Legal structure

In what legal form will you do business?

Why is this form best for you?

If more than one person is in the business, include agreements.

Insurance

What insurance will your business carry?

Management

How will your business be managed on a day-to-day basis?

Who will be responsible for monthly financial reports?

How will management change in the future?

How will your business records be maintained?

Advisors

Who is your accountant?

Who is your attorney?

Who are the people you can turn to for good advice?

Other issues

Discuss any other issues pertinent to your business.

4. Financial plan

Start-up capital

What equipment or supplies will you need?

What are your resources?

What financing will you need?

Cash-flow projections

Monthly: Use "best guess," "high side," and "low side" numbers.

Purpose and amount of the loan

An exact dollar amount you want to borrow for the business and a description of how you will use the money.

Explanation of your personal credit

If you have had any credit problems, acknowledge them and explain how you have resolved them.

Summing Up

Ready to get started? After reading though the business plan outline, you may think that it asks for more information than you have. This workbook will help you gather the necessary information and make decisions based on that information. Learning is like building with blocks. What you learn at first determines which questions you need to answer next. In the next chapter, you consider what business would be best for you, and we explain how you can share your business dream with others so they can share your excitement.

CHAPTER 2

Defining Your Dream

Some people are very clear about the type of business they want to start. But it's perfectly acceptable to first decide that you want to start a business and then brainstorm and research the kind of business that would work for you. A good way to begin the process is to think about who you are, what you enjoy doing, and how you really want to spend your time.

After you decide what kind of business you want, take time to daydream and develop a clear mental image of your business. Imagine yourself doing the business. This is the first step in communicating your idea to others. Write a brief description of your business and practice saying it. Select a name for your business; giving it a name will make it feel more real.

In this chapter, you identify the business you want to start and the people who can support you in this new adventure. It is important to know who those people are *before* you need them.

A Good Business for You

To get started, read through, think about, and then answer the following questions:

What are your gifts and talents? A gift is anything you do very well or something that comes easily to you.

_____

_____

_____

What are your passions? Is there something you feel so strongly about that you want to spend your time convincing others of its worth?

_____

_____

_____

What business ideas have you read or heard about that interest you? Spend some time reading and learning about businesses others are starting. Be open to new ideas.

_____

_____

_____

What are your personal goals? Be sure to consider your lifestyle. It's important to select a business that satisfies you and involves work you love and do well.

_____

_____

_____

For some people, life just goes around and around. They work, pay bills, and deal with family and friends day after day and year after year. Many people don't take time to daydream or if they do, they never tell anyone or take any action on their dreams. When we were young, we knew how to daydream, and nothing was impossible. If we take the time, we can relearn how to daydream.

Every successful business starts as a daydream in the owner's mind. The time you spend imagining yourself making your product or delivering your service and actually running your business is time well spent. Some people have such strong, vivid images of their businesses that they are practically compelled to start them. So get comfortable, close your eyes, and "see" your business. Take time to dream every day until your thoughts begin to seem possible and real. Keep a daydreaming notebook so you can jot your ideas down. Use the following questions to get started, and when you have the answers, write them in.

Where to Find Business Ideas

- The public library
- The Internet
- Entrepreneurial magazines
- Newspapers, radio, and television
- Friends, relatives, or acquaintances
- The Yellow Pages

What is my business dream?

_____

_____

_____

Where is my place of business? What am I doing? Am I using a computer or other equipment?

_____

_____

_____

Who are my customers?

_____

_____

_____

What is my typical workday like?

_____

_____

_____

Business Ideas

List the business possibilities you are considering. List the advantages and disadvantages of each business. Consider start-up costs, hours, the type of work, and any other factors you can think of.

Business Idea	Advantages	Disadvantages

35 Business Ideas to Consider

Alterations/Seamstress

Antiques dealer

Auto detailing

Bookkeeping

Child care provider

Consulting

Craft business

Desktop publishing

Dog training

Editor

Elder care

Event-planning service

Financial aid service

Gift basket service

Graphic designer

Handyman service

Home computer operator

Home health care

Home inspection service

House painter

Import/Export business guide

Information broker

Landscaper

Mail order business

Medical claims processing

Personal trainer

Pet sitting

Photographer

Professional organizer

Retail

Secretarial/Word processing

Software designer

Tour guide

Vending machine business

Web designer

Exploring Your Dreams

Once you have a list of possible business ideas, there is other important work to do. You need to take time to know yourself, define your values, and research your choices to make certain that your business is a good fit for you.

Know Yourself

Starting a business is a wonderful time to get honest about who you are. Better self aware-ness can help you consider which daydreams are best suited for your personality. The fol-lowing exercise can get you started:

Explain yourself in terms of your strengths, attitudes, and self-image. What do others think of you? What do you do well? What are your weaknesses? Try not to define yourself in terms of what you own or the roles you play (mother, husband, daughter, etc.).

In the space below, write a short description of who you are. Be honest. This inventory may be uncomfortable, but it is necessary if you want to make good decisions.

_____

_____

_____

Define Your Values

Values—also called principles, ideals, purposes, beliefs, and convictions—are your most important fundamental beliefs. Your values determine how you treat people, the relation-ships you seek, and your ideas of right and wrong. Values are your fundamental convic-tions and they are directly tied to how you make your living. You make choices every day about how you will spend your money and how you spend your time. Consider those choices as you define your value system.

Have you ever dreamed for months about going on a great vacation and then had that vacation be a miserable experience? The same thing can happen if the decisions in your life are not based on your personal values. The outcome may leave you feeling dissatisfied.

It is important that your business be operated by and in tune with your core values. Use the next two questions to articulate your value system:

What three values would you want people to identify with you?

_____

_____

_____

What values will motivate the way you do business?

_____

_____

_____

Research Your Choices

You may have eliminated some of the daydream businesses on your list as you considered your personality and/or your value system. Take the business ideas that remain and list the pros and cons of each. Get educated about the issues that are related to your business of interest. Look at practical things, such as the amount of money it would take to start the business, the amount of money you could make, the hours that would be required, the type of customers you would deal with, and the type of work involved. Keep an open mind while you research, and don't feel pressured to make a final decision too quickly.

Narrow Your Choices

Talk to people in the selected businesses. Here are some questions you should ask the owner of each business:

- How did you get into this business?
- What is a typical day like in your business?
- What was the biggest surprise you learned after starting the business?
- If you had to start your business over, what would you do differently?

Read about those businesses. Try to find statistics about the businesses. How profitable are they? Are they stable? Are they difficult to manage?

Ask your accountant or your banker about select businesses. Here are some questions you should consider asking:

- Do you have other clients in the same or similar business?
- What struggles have you noticed with these clients?
- What do you see as the biggest challenge to this business?
- How can you help me overcome these challenges?

Share your ideas with family and friends and be ready to listen to their reactions. Be aware of the impact that your decision could have on them.

Make a decision about which business to investigate further.

In later chapters, we discuss how to determine if your business idea will work. But at this beginning stage, the best thing you can do is talk through your idea. Be prepared to listen carefully to people's reactions. Try not to take comments personally; instead, use the feedback to determine if your business idea should be modified or even discarded or if you should continue your investigation. And don't be discouraged if you dismiss several business ideas before finding one that seems possible. Be prepared to take your time and think through each idea. To investigate a business, you must learn and listen; fortunately, both are inexpensive activities.

Create a "Sound-Bite" for Your Business

Politicians use a "sound-bite" to answer complex questions. They know they have only a few moments to describe a very complicated issue. They can't go into detail but must give a concise, precise answer that will lead to more discussion.

The same technique works for small business owners. While family and friends may have the time to work through long descriptions of your proposed business, investors and loan officers do not. And, of course, in today's fast-paced world, customers will seldom give you more than 20 seconds of their time. Developing a "sound-bite" for your business idea is good practice for the future.

Spend time thinking through how you will explain your business idea to others. If you want someone to listen to your idea and react to it, you must be very clear in what you say. Practice your description often so you can present your business dream clearly in just one or two sentences when you have an opportunity.

Communication Exercise

Read through the dialogue below. Imagine the patient friend's reaction to the business starter's rambling answer to the question "What is your new business?"

Business Starter: "I'm going to start a new business!"

Patient Friend: "Oh, really? What is your new business?"

Business Starter: "Well, **you know how**, have you ever thought about, um, starting to do something different in your life? You know, like when your job is a drag and your boss is a jerk and you aren't making any money, so you decide to start your own business—but, you know, think about how **difficult it would be if you decided that you wanted to go into business for yourself but you had no idea**, absolutely no idea. I mean, how would you? How would you know, even, **where to begin?** Huh? Well, you wouldn't, because how many times before have you ever gone into business for yourself? Really! Think about it—it would be a totally foreign experience. Okay! So **even if you went to the library and read books about it, most of that material is written**, and I know this for a fact, it's written **in business language, which most people don't understand.** So, my idea would be, I mean, if people thought it would work—I'd have to ask a lot of people if they thought it would—but if a lot of people thought it might work, **my business** idea **would** be to **provide training to people who have no idea how to start a business of their own.** After all, I've had my own business before, so I have some experience in this, and I have a friend who has had a couple of businesses, and she could help me. **And my training would be in plain English, using words everyone can understand,** because, after all, I know I'm a good communicator. I mean, don't you feel bad for people who really want to quit their jobs and would if they could, but they just don't know how to...they just don't know where to begin to, **and,** anyway, **I would base the training around writing a business plan,** and we could talk about—and this would be really cool!—experiences other people have had starting their own businesses. And I would provide, you know, resource materials about how to name your business, and I could teach people about marketing and financial stuff, and all kinds of stuff that people would need to know but don't know, you know?"

Impatient Friend: "So...have you met that new guy in accounting?"

Now, go through the dialogue again, this time reading only the bold sections of the business starter's answer. What might the friend's reaction be now?

Even when your business is still just a daydream, it's important to practice describing it as concisely and precisely as possible. Entrepreneurs tend to get excited and give too much information that confuses the listener. Most listeners that matter—those you are trying to convince of the value of your business idea—are primarily interested in the answers to only a few key questions. You can start to define your business by answering them:

- What problem does your business solve?
- Who needs your solution?
- How is the problem being solved now?
- What can you do to set your business apart?

Here is another good exercise. Imagine you get onto an elevator with a stranger and you both push the tenth floor button. After greeting you, the person asks "What do you do for a living?" You have just a few seconds to respond with an answer that will spark interest and make the stranger ask more questions about your business. What do you say?

_____

_____

_____

_____

Now make a list of people with whom you want to share your business idea. Start with people you know who are supportive of you. Jot down their reactions. As you are more comfortable with presenting your sound bite, share it with your accountant, banker, and attorney.

Person	Reaction
_____	_____
_____	_____
_____	_____
_____	_____

What's in a Name?

Everyone knows how important a name can be, whether you're talking about a baby or a new business. We all know businesses with great names (and businesses with so-so names). Be prepared to spend time finding the right name for your business. As you gather information about your business, keep tossing names around in your head and write them down. Take time to select the best name for your business, because whatever you choose, you'll have to live with it. Make sure the name you select meets most of these criteria:

- It quickly identifies what you do.
- It stands out from the competition.
- It's easy to remember.
- It's easy to spell and pronounce.
- It's neither too short nor too long.

First, brainstorm a long list of adjectives that describe what you want your business to reflect. What are some special features of your business? Think of words or phrases that tell what the business does, communicate the primary benefit of your product or service, or describe the main activity of your business. Next, piece the words together. How do they sound together? Do they convey the image you want for your business? Will your customers remember the name?

Share the best names with friends. Listen to their reactions. Don't panic if you don't have the perfect name as you begin planning your business. As you gather information and your dream becomes more real to you, the right name will come to you.

Identify Your Support Team

The decision to start a new business is yours to make, but it's important to identify people who will be supportive *before* you begin your business. Although financial support is obviously helpful, you should also think about who in your life will give you emotional support, objective critiques, and new ideas. You need people around you who believe in your dream and your ability to realize it. Having people offer enthusiastic support, helpful suggestions, and consistent encouragement greatly increases your likelihood of success.

Who are the supportive people in your life?

_____

_____

_____

Starting a business is a major life change, and even though the change is positive, it will be stressful. You also are creating major changes for your family, and their fears and concerns may make it difficult for them to be supportive all the time. It is important to listen to their concerns but to also share your need for their support. It is equally important to look for other sources of support among your network of extended family, friends, and business associates. The more people you have behind you, the greater your chances for success.

Summing Up

The first step in developing a clear mental image of your business is to consider your gifts, talents, and interests. Take the time to daydream. Once you have it in mind, be certain to clearly communicate your business idea to people and identify friends or family who will be supportive. In the next chapter, we look at the next step toward making your dreams come true: getting them financed.

CHAPTER 3

Financing the Dream

Financing your business can be a difficult task. Before you approach a lender, it's important to understand the lending process and to be well prepared.

In this chapter, you learn the language of finance and read about the Four Ps of Finance and Five Cs of Lending. You also look at your credit options and what you need to do to finance your dream.

A Look at Your Business

Answer the following questions to begin thinking of ways to finance your business:

1. Do you personally have enough money to finance your business dream?

   Yes_____   No_____

   If you checked No, answer the questions below.

2. How much money (in cash, equipment, and inventory) can you invest in your business?

   _____

3. Do family or friends have money they are willing to invest in your business?

   Yes_____   No_____   If so, how much? _____

4. If you and your family and friends cannot invest enough, how much money do you need to borrow to start a new business or maintain your existing business?

   _____

5. Write down how you would use invested or borrowed money in your business:

Amount	Purpose
$ _____	_____
$ _____	_____
$ _____	_____
$ _____	_____
$ _____	_____
$ _____	_____
$ _____	_____

6. Where can you go to borrow this money?

   _____

Financing 101

The dream of being self-employed is an exciting one, but a common obstacle to realizing that dream is a lack of money. Even if you succeed in starting a business, getting a loan to maintain or grow it is often necessary and sometimes difficult.

Before you seek money for your business dream, you should understand the basics of financing. In the rest of the chapter, we look at the reality of grants for small businesses, what a lender considers when reviewing a loan request, some common financial terms, how to identify essential business needs, how to create a financial plan, and why it's important to develop a relationship with your lender. We also review the loan application process, personal credit reports, and what you can expect if your loan request is approved.

Before turning to the steps of financing a business, take a look at some common financial terms.

The Language of Finance

- **Capital** is the money, equipment, or other major contribution invested to start a business. Capital typically is not recovered until a business is sold. Capital usually comes from two sources: investors (including the business owner) and lenders.

  - **Equity capital** is money the business owner or other people invest. Equity capital carries with it a share of ownership and, usually, a share in the profits.

  - **Debt capital** is money an owner borrows to start a business. This money must be repaid to the lender with interest.

- **Equity (or net worth)** is what remains when everything a company owes (its *liabilities*) is subtracted from everything a company owns (its *assets*). Equity can be greater than or less than the amount of capital invested in the business.

- **Collateral** is something of value the borrower owns and is willing to pledge as a secondary method of repayment if he or she fails to repay the loan in cash. The lender *secures* (lays claim to) the collateral at the time the loan is made so that no other lender can secure the same collateral during the life of the loan.

- A **loan** is money that is borrowed and must be repaid, usually under specified terms and conditions. There are three common types of loans:

  - **Short-term loans** provide money for short periods of time, usually 30 to 90 days. The original amount you borrow and must repay is called the *principal*. The fee charged for borrowing the money is called *interest*. In a short-term note, the money is used for the term of the note; then principal plus interest is repaid all at once.

  - A **line of credit** is an approved amount of money a borrower can access as needed. The repayment on a line of credit is established at the beginning of the loan. Repayment terms are flexible and may include monthly interest-only payments and quarterly or annual principal repayments.

  - **Long-term loans** often are used to buy real estate or equipment, and the purchased item is secured for collateral. (That is, the lender retains ownership of the real estate or the equipment until the loan is paid back.) Long-term loans have repayment terms of more than 12 months. Monthly payments are made, with a portion applied to interest and the remainder applied to the principal.

- **Working capital** is the amount of money available to pay short-term expenses. It's like a cushion to meet unexpected or out-of-the-ordinary expenses. A working capital loan can help a start-up business pay operating expenses for a short time as the business becomes self-sustaining. To get this kind of loan, a financial plan must show a business's ability to reach sustainability in a reasonable period of time.

The Risky Start-Up

The business owner stands to benefit the most from (and has the most control over) a business's success. Because of this, the owner is expected to assume the most risk when starting a business. Start-up businesses usually are financed through the personal resources of the business owner: savings, investments, equity in a home, and loans or investments from family and friends.

Sometimes, the entrepreneur must find a lender willing to finance the start-up. However, financing a business start-up is the riskiest loan a lender can make. A start-up business doesn't exist, so the owner cannot demonstrate its capacity to make a profit (and repay the loan). Even if the entrepreneur has significant experience producing the same product or service, being a successful entrepreneur requires a different set of skills.

For example, entrepreneurs must market and sell their products or services. They must manage cash flow daily, keep accurate records, understand financial reports, and use the reports to make informed decisions. They must set prices that are not too high or too low. Entrepreneurs must relate well to customers, employees, suppliers, and creditors. In time, successful entrepreneurs develop strong business management skills, but mistakes are often made along the way. The magnitude of those mistakes can mean the difference between success and failure.

That lender is taking a chance on the unproven abilities of the entrepreneur, often a person not well known to the lender. It is in the best interests of the entrepreneur to develop an honest relationship with the lender. The entrepreneur must provide sufficient convincing information that the business start-up represents a worthy risk. The lender has to believe in the business idea and trust the entrepreneur. That trust must be earned, and building trust takes time.

Avoiding Debt

Can you start a business without going into debt? Many successful business owners do. Consider starting small and growing your business over time. Concentrate your efforts on increasing sales and building a loyal client base. Keep profits in the business instead of raising your salary as revenues go up. By making some concessions in the beginning, you may be able to build the business of your dreams without incurring debt.

The Existing Business

Is it any easier to get credit after a business owner has gathered enough resources to start a small business? The answer depends on a number of factors: the owner's relationship with the lender, the financial strength of the business, the way the owner manages the business, the borrower's ability to repay the loan, and the existence of an alternative method of repaying the loan if the business isn't as profitable as the owner projected.

Sometimes, a business owner approaches a lender only after the business is in financial crisis. The owner then is desperately seeking cash as a short-term solution to a significant problem, often with no long-range plans to keep the problem from reoccurring. This owner is unlikely to get a loan. Lenders prefer to develop long-term relationships with business owners who take the time—and have the ability—to manage their businesses well.

A borrower needs a clear idea of how much money the business needs and how the money will be used to maintain the business. If the borrower cannot explain these things clearly to the lender, the loan request likely will be denied. A lender is looking for a plan that explains how the money being borrowed will be invested to strengthen the business or, in other words, how the loan will help the business generate the additional income required to repay the loan.

It is important to prove that the business is borrowing enough money but not too much money. For example, a business may need money to buy equipment that will significantly increase its capacity to produce a product. With proper planning, increased production should result in increased sales. If the owner borrows too little, the equipment cannot be purchased. The borrowed money might be spent on operating costs until the funds are depleted. In the end, the business is left with no increase in sales and a debt it cannot repay. Likewise, a business that borrows too much money may not increase its sales enough to generate the cash required to repay the loan. The key to determining how much money your business should borrow is proper planning.

The "Free Money" Myth

There is a common misconception that a person who wants to launch a small or home-based business can easily apply for and receive "free" federal grant money to do so. This is simply not the case. Grants are sometimes awarded to "small" for-profit businesses that meet the size standards established by the U.S. Small Business Administration (SBA), but some of these standards include 100 employees for wholesale trade businesses, 500 employees for most manufacturing and mining businesses, and $6 million in annual revenue for most retail and service businesses! In other words, the majority of small business start-ups don't qualify.

In addition, the SBA's grant programs generally support nonprofit organizations; intermediary lending institutions; and state and local governments that provide management, technical, or financial assistance to small businesses. The SBA does not offer grants to start or expand small businesses directly.

The SBA *does* offer a wide variety of lending programs to assist small business, but it is primarily a guarantor of loans. This means that a bank or lending institution actually makes the loan to the small business owner and the SBA guarantees it in case the borrower *defaults on* (fails to repay) the loan. This guarantee allows banks to make loans they otherwise wouldn't agree to make.

With an SBA guarantee, the borrower may expect to pay a higher interest rate as well as some fees; still, the SBA guarantee may enable a borrower to get a loan that he or she might not be approved for otherwise. For example, a business owner with limited resources to invest in his or her business or one hoping to launch a start-up business is not likely to qualify for a bank loan without an SBA guarantee. To qualify for an SBA loan guarantee, the borrower must have a completed business plan. He or she should have some financial investment in the business and must meet a minimum credit score requirement. For more information on SBA loan programs along with a list of local resources, visit the SBA Web site at www.sba.gov/services.

Getting a Loan

The steps in this section help you go through the process of obtaining a loan to finance your business.

Identify Your Needs

The first step in financing your business is to identify your needs. Don't think in terms of dollars; think in terms of what your business needs to get started or to grow. For example, do you need to buy equipment or inventory? Are you looking for a way to test your market? Answer the following questions as you think about your start-up needs:

1. Will you need to rent or buy space for your business? If so, what costs will be associated with that space?

    a. Lease deposit $_____

    b. Utility deposits $_____

    c. Build-out costs: materials + labor $_____

    d. Landscaping $_____

    e. Signage + installation $_____

    f. Furniture + delivery $_____

    g. Display units/fixtures + installation $_____

    h. Decorating costs $_____

    i. Insurance $_____

2. Will you need to purchase equipment for your business? If so, what kind of equipment and how much will it cost? Don't forget to include shipping or freight costs.

    _____

    _____

    _____

3. What professional fees will you incur before opening your business?

    a. Attorney fees $_____

    b. Accounting fees $_____

    c. Association dues, subscriptions $_____

    d. Business insurance $_____

4. What will you need for supplies and inventory?

    a. Start-up inventory $_____

    b. Office supplies $_____

    c. Cleaning + misc supplies $_____

5. How much will you spend for advertising and related expenses?

    a. Advertising $_____

    b. Web site design + related costs $_____

    c. Letterhead, business cards, flyers, brochures, etc. $_____

When you have a list of your needs, examine it carefully and ask yourself this question: Is everything on the list essential? To determine the answer, identify those items that will generate money for your business and those that won't. Say, for example, you own an alterations business and you need a new sewing machine. Clearly, the sewing machine will generate income for your business: It's essential. A new cell phone might be convenient and a leather desk chair might be nice, but they won't generate income for your business: They are not essential.

Use your judgment to separate essential and nonessential items. For example, you might be able to operate your business inexpensively from your home. But if your customers expect your business to be located in an office or storefront, then renting space might be the only way to succeed.

After you have listed your essential needs, it's time to calculate their cost. You must request a loan amount that finances essential items and makes sense for your business. Don't begin the financing process with a vague dollar amount in mind, and don't base your request on how much you think you can borrow. Instead, do some research and list your actual start-up costs.

Develop a Financial Plan

The next step is creating a financial plan. Your plan will show the loan money coming into your business and your "essential needs" purchases being made. It will show money coming in from sales and money going out to pay expenses. Of course, it will show your business repaying the loan over a specific period of time. There are a few things a lender will want to see in your plan:

- **The projections must seem reasonable.** If you are financing a start-up business and you project high sales from the first day, your projections may not be realistic. In most businesses, sales start slowly and increase over time.

- **If your business will have seasonal fluctuations, these should be reflected in the plan.** A business that sells Christmas trees may have sales in November and December and none the rest of the year.

- **Finally, your operating expenses and the salary you take out must relate to the scale of your business.** Don't estimate your salary at $100,000 per year for a small mowing business with only one mower. Your projections must make sense given the size and scale of your business.

In Exercise #1, you will review two financial plans prepared for Dave's Lawn-Mowing Service. Try to think like a loan officer. Which plan seems like the best bet for your financial institution?

Exercise #1

Dave wants to borrow $2,000 to start a lawn-mowing service. He plans to start the business in January, operate the business part time, and have no employees. Review Dave's first financial plan below and then answer the questions that follow.

Dave's Lawn-Mowing Service

Six-Month Financial Plan #1
Loan Request: $2,000
Business Start-Up Date: January 1

Cash In	Start-Up	Jan	Feb	Mar	Apr	May	Jun	Total
Loan proceeds	$2,000							$2,000
Lawn-mowing income		$1,500	$1,500	$1,500	$1,500	$1,500	$1,500	$9,000
Total Cash In	$2,000	$1,500	$1,500	$1,500	$1,500	$1,500	$1,500	$11,000
Cash Out								
Lawn mower	$1,500							$1,500
Gas & oil for mower		$350	$350	$350	$350	$350	$350	$2,100
Truck expenses		$250	$250	$250	$250	$250	$250	$1,500
Advertising		$100	$100	$100	$100	$100	$100	$600
Insurance		$25	$25	$25	$25	$25	$25	$150
Loan payments		$0	$175	$175	$175	$175	$175	$875
Owner's salary	$500	$775	$600	$600	$600	$600	$600	$4,275
Total Cash Out	$2,000	$1,500	$1,500	$1,500	$1,500	$1,500	$1,500	$11,000
Remaining Cash Balance	**$0**	**$0**	**$0**	**$0**	**$0**	**$0**	**$0**	**$0**

1. Does Dave's plan seem realistic? Yes_____ No_____ Why? _____

   _____

   _____

2. How does Dave plan to use the loan money?_____

   _____

3. Does Dave include a plan to repay the loan? Yes_____ No_____

4. Do Dave's sales projections seem reasonable? Yes_____ No_____

   Is his salary reasonable? Yes_____ No_____

   Do his expenses seem reasonable? Yes_____ No_____

5. How could Dave improve this financial plan?_____

   _____

6. Based on this financial plan, would you loan Dave the $2,000 he is requesting?

   Yes_____ No_____

(continued)

(continued)

Dave has revised his business idea. Notice that in his revised plan, Dave has decided to wait until April 1 to start his new business. Review Dave's revised plan below and then answer the questions that follow.

Dave's Lawn-Mowing Service

Six-Month Financial Plan #2
Loan Request: $2,000
Business Start-Up Date: April 1

Cash In	Start-Up	Apr	May	Jun	Jul	Aug	Sep	Total
Loan proceeds	$2,000							$2,000
Lawn-mowing income		$350	$450	$550	$650	$800	$800	$3,600
Total Cash In	$2,000	$350	$450	$550	$650	$800	$800	$5,600
Cash Out								
Lawn mower	$1,500							$1,500
Gas & oil for mower		$35	$45	$55	$65	$80	$80	$360
Truck expenses		$53	$67	$83	$97	$120	$120	$540
Advertising		$50	$50	$50	$50	$50	$25	$275
Insurance		$25	$25	$25	$25	$25	$25	$150
Loan payments		$175	$175	$175	$175	$175	$175	$1,050
Owner's salary	$0	$50	$100	$150	$200	$325	$400	$1,225
Total Cash Out	$1,500	$388	$462	$538	$612	$775	$825	$5,100
Remaining Cash Balance	**$500**	**$462**	**$450**	**$462**	**$500**	**$525**	**$500**	**$500**

1. Does this plan seem more reasonable than the first? Yes_____ No_____ Why?_____

_____

_____

2. How does Dave plan to use the loan money?_____

_____

3. Does Dave include a plan to repay the loan? Yes_____ No_____

4. Do Dave's sales projections seem reasonable? Yes_____ No_____

Is his salary reasonable? Yes_____ No_____

Do his expenses seem reasonable? Yes_____ No_____

5. How could Dave improve this financial plan?_____

_____

6. Based on this financial plan, would you loan Dave the $2,000 he is requesting?

Yes_____ No_____

The Application Process

Loan application requirements vary among lenders. You probably will be required to submit a business plan (or at least an executive summary) that describes the products or services you will sell, short- and long-term goals for your business, information about you and your management staff, your marketing strategy, and financial information.

When you are using your business plan to get financing, you should include a specific financing request. The financing request, or *use of funds statement,* is simply a breakdown of how you propose to use the loan. The use of funds statement should be as detailed as possible, including equipment, model numbers, descriptions, and prices. Include catalogs or brochures describing the equipment you want to buy. Remember that your use of funds statement must be supported by the financial plan you submit. Here is an example of a use of funds statement:

Use of Funds Statement

Equipment:	High-speed Laser Printer Model 5400 (see brochure attached)	$1,000
Advertising:	Town Crier Newspaper, ½" display ads for 4 weeks	
	Radio advertising 30-second spots (see details attached)	$500
Working Capital		$1,000
Total Loan Request		**$2,500**

Your lender probably has a loan application packet. Pick up the packet and take it home with you. Fill it out neatly and completely. Don't forget to attach any additional information the lender requests, such as personal financial statements or tax returns. *If you have questions, ask them.* If you or your business have issues that may be of concern to your lender, don't try to hide them: Bring them up when you make your loan request and address them honestly.

The Five Cs of Lending

Following are the Five Cs of lending, which are considerations a loan officer makes while reviewing your credit application. Be prepared to answer questions and provide information about these five Cs:

- **Good Character:** The owner's personal integrity
- **Capacity:** The company's financial strength and ability to repay its debt
- **Capital:** How much debt the company has compared to its equity
- **Collateral:** A secondary source of repayment
- **Conditions:** The conditions of the economy and the industry

Get to Know Your Lender

While you are in the early stages of identifying your needs and creating your financial plan, begin establishing a relationship with your lender. Stop in and say hello. Introduce yourself. Tell the lender you are in the planning stages of financing a business. Don't take a lot of his or her time talking about your business idea before you're ready to make your loan request. Simply let the lender know who you are and that you intend to approach him or her when you are ready.

The Four Ps of Finance

- **Preparation:** Be thorough when preparing your business plan, and be prepared when you approach lenders and investors.

- **Presentation:** You must be ready and able to sell yourself and your business to others. Practice with friends before you approach lenders and investors.

- **Positive attitude:** You must project confidence in yourself and in your business. A positive attitude comes from thorough preparation, practice, and a strong belief in your ability to succeed.

- **Persistence:** This might be the most important ingredient in getting financing. Prepare to be turned down several times before you succeed. If you are turned down, ask yourself some questions: How can I make this work? What can I change to get the financing I need? Finding money is not always easy, but it is possible!

It's also a good idea to do your personal banking at the institution where you plan to request your loan. If you have a separate business checking account, some banks require that you keep it with them. And don't do your banking at the drive-through window. Go into the office, stop by the loan officer's desk, and say hello.

Remember, business is about relationships. People do business with people they know and like. Whether yours is a start-up or an existing business, begin a relationship with the lender well before you need a loan. After all, you'll be asking the lender to share a financial risk with you, and your working relationship will last a long time. So let the loan officer get to know you. Be a familiar face!

Personal Credit

We don't want to scare you, but someone has been watching you. Each time you've signed for a car loan, used a credit card, or taken out a mortgage, the activity has been reported to a credit bureau. If you have a history of making late payments, it shows up on your personal credit report. If you have failed to repay a loan as promised, had a court judgment against you, had any tax liens filed against you, or filed personal bankruptcy within the last 10 years, it shows up on your credit report.

But there's good news, as well: If you have made your payments on time, repaid your debts as promised, and have a track record of being a reliable credit risk, that shows up on your credit report, too! When you request financing for your business, lenders will require you to sign forms that allow them to obtain your personal credit report. Your personal credit is a major consideration, even when you are applying for a business loan.

(Your lender is taking a risk on you as well as your business.) Your credit report tells a story about you, and you should know what the story is before you apply for a loan.

Order your own credit report at least once a year, and check it for accuracy. Sometimes credit bureaus make mistakes, and other people's credit transactions can show up on your report. You can ask a credit bureau to correct errors on your report by filing the appropriate paperwork. Be prepared to prove your claims. If you have difficulty getting a credit bureau to remove an item from your report, you can at least have them note that the entry is in dispute. If you are (or were) married and you and your spouse have (or had) joint accounts, each of your credit reports will include those accounts.

Your report may show a poor credit history at a time when you experienced some hardship, such as a divorce or a medical catastrophe. Most credit bureaus allow you to submit a short narrative explaining the circumstances of poor or questionable credit. This narrative will appear when a creditor requests a copy of your credit history. Many lenders are willing to take hardships into consideration when reviewing your credit, but you should address the issue up front: Tell them what they will find before they find it, and be honest.

If your report reflects a recent period of poor or no repayment, your lender will look for indications that you are trying to rebuild your credit. Following are some strategies for reestablishing a good credit history:

- **Get help from a nonprofit consumer credit counseling agency.** These agencies help you get copies of your credit history, correct reporting errors, and establish a plan to rebuild your credit.

- **Get a secured credit card.** This is a card that is tied to a savings account that you deposit a sum of money into. Your deposit becomes the line of credit for that account.

- **Pay off delinquent accounts as soon as possible.** This will not remove the negative item from your credit report, but a late payment is not as bad as an unpaid debt.

- **Start paying your bills on time.** The older a late payment is, the less it hurts your score. And ask that negative information older than 7 years (10 years for a bankruptcy) be removed from your credit report.

- **Avoid credit repair companies.** While you can have errors removed from your report, you cannot legitimately "fix" items that are true. Some credit repair companies run a scam where they charge you a fee to dispute every item on your credit report. The credit bureau temporarily removes the items from your report while they investigate them. The credit repair company will then show you a "clean" report with the negative items removed. Unfortunately, once the credit bureau verifies that the entries are legitimate, they reappear on your report. Your credit report will not be repaired but your wallet will be considerably lighter!

You've Been Approved! Now What?

If your loan request is approved, your lender may write a commitment letter that outlines the terms and conditions of the loan. Your lender will schedule a loan closing, at which time you will sign the documents required by the lender and receive your loan proceeds. Typical loan documents include these:

- **A promissory note:** When you sign this note, you promise to repay the loan under the specified terms.

- **A security agreement:** By signing this, you give the lender a secured interest in the collateral you have pledged.

- **A personal guaranty:** Lenders usually require the owner(s) of a business to personally guarantee the loan. This means that if the business is unable to repay the loan for any reason, the owner(s) agree to assume personal responsibility for repayment.

Read all the loan documents carefully, and ask questions about anything you don't understand before you sign anything.

Your lender may charge closing fees to help cover the administrative costs of the loan. Ask about closing fees before the closing. Fees can be paid by the borrower at the closing, deducted from the loan proceeds, or added to the balance of the loan.

An Interest in You!

Lenders are businesses, and they cover their operating and administrative expenses by charging interest on loans. *Interest* is the fee the borrower pays in exchange for access to credit. Interest typically is charged according to an annual percentage rate (APR): If your annual interest rate is 12 percent, you will be charged 1 percent interest (one-twelfth) on the balance of your loan each month. Below is an amortization schedule that shows the principal and interest breakdown of each monthly payment. Your lender can explain how interest and principal are calculated on your loan.

Amortization Schedule

Loan Date: 26-Jan-2XXX
Amount: $2,000.00
Interest Rate: 12.00%
Term: 24 months
Payment Amount: $94.15

Payment #	Due Date	Beg Bal	Amt Paid	Interest	Principal	Ending Bal
1	01-Mar	$2,000.00	$94.15	$20.00	$74.15	$1,925.85
2	01-Apr	$1,925.85	$94.15	$19.26	$74.89	$1,850.96
3	01-May	$1,850.96	$94.15	$18.51	$75.64	$1,775.32
4	01-Jun	$1,775.32	$94.15	$17.75	$76.39	$1,698.93
5	01-Jul	$1,698.93	$94.15	$16.99	$77.16	$1,621.77
6	01-Aug	$1,621.77	$94.15	$16.22	$77.93	$1,543.84
7	01-Sep	$1,543.84	$94.15	$15.44	$78.71	$1,465.13
8	01-Oct	$1,465.13	$94.15	$14.65	$79.50	$1,385.63
9	01-Nov	$1,385.63	$94.15	$13.86	$80.29	$1,305.34
10	01-Dec	$1,305.34	$94.15	$13.05	$81.09	$1,224.25
11	01-Jan	$1,224.25	$94.15	$12.24	$81.90	$1,142.35
12	01-Feb	$1,142.35	$94.15	$11.42	$82.72	$1,059.63
13	01-Mar	$1,059.63	$94.15	$10.60	$83.55	$976.08
14	01-Apr	$967.08	$94.15	$9.76	$84.39	$891.69
15	01-May	$891.69	$94.15	$8.92	$85.23	$806.46
16	01-Jun	$806.46	$94.15	$8.06	$86.08	$720.38
17	01-Jul	$720.38	$94.15	$7.20	$86.94	$633.44

Payment #	Due Date	Beg Bal	Amt Paid	Interest	Principal	Ending Bal
18	01-Aug	$633.44	$94.15	$6.33	$87.81	$545.63
19	01-Sep	$545.63	$94.15	$5.46	$88.69	$456.94
20	01-Oct	$456.94	$94.15	$4.57	$89.58	$367.36
21	01-Nov	$367.36	$94.15	$3.67	$90.47	$276.89
22	01-Dec	$276.89	$94.15	$2.77	$91.38	$185.51
23	01-Jan	$185.51	$94.15	$1.86	$92.29	$93.22
24	01-Feb	$93.22	$94.15	$0.93	$93.22	($0.00)
	Total:	**$2,000.00**	**$2,259.53**	**$259.53**	**$2,000.00**	**($0.00)**

Ending Balance = Beginning Balance – Principal

Summing Up

Making small business loans is a risky proposition for lenders. When you apply for a small business loan, be prepared to answer questions and make a strong argument that you and your business have the ability to repay the loan. To be adequately prepared, you should

- Identify the essential items you need to start, strengthen, or grow your business.
- Create a realistic financial plan that demonstrates how the loan proceeds will be used and how your business will repay the loan.
- Include all the essential information the lender will need to make a decision, such as a detailed use of funds statement and the manufacturer's information about any equipment you propose to buy.
- Be aware of what your personal credit history says about you. If there are errors on your credit report, correct them before applying for your loan. If there are issues that require an explanation, be prepared to honestly address them with your lender.
- Understand the terms of the loan and be prepared to ask the lender questions.

Now that you have a better idea of how you will finance your business, it's time to set some specific goals for making it a success.

CHAPTER 4

Set Goals So You Take Action

In Chapter 2, we said that the first step to creating a business is to have a dream and then define it. Yet have you ever noticed how many people talk about their dream but never act on it? They talk about the same dream for years or they may change the dream from time to time, but they never take steps to realize it. These people never move beyond daydreaming to the next stage: setting goals.

Once you've taken the time to know yourself, define your values, and research your choices, you're ready to set your goals. You'll know it's time to set goals when you want to make changes more than you want things to stay the same. In this chapter, we will discuss how to set a goal and then create an action plan. If you have a solid goal and a well-thought-out action plan, you'll greatly increase your chances of making your daydream a reality.

Set a Goal

We all have experience reaching a goal because we have all made things happen in our lives, like graduating from high school or college, losing weight, paying off bills, or learning to dance. Think of something you have accomplished that you are proud of.

What was your accomplishment? _____

_____

_____

What steps did you take to achieve this? _____

_____

_____

_____

_____

Most people would agree that setting goals is an important step in fulfilling dreams, yet only 3% of Americans actually write down their life goals and monitor them. The process of setting goals is not complicated, but it does require you to be honest with yourself and do some serious thinking about what you really want to achieve.

Keep in mind that successful people not only set goals, they use these goals to make decisions and keep themselves focused. So in this chapter we go through the process of naming your goals and then using them to stay focused on what you really want from life.

Establishing Effective Goals

Any farmer can tell you that when you plow a field, you must keep your eyes fixed on one point on the horizon. Without that fixed point, your row will meander all over the field. The same is true in life. If you don't keep a specific target in sight, you'll wander off course. Keep the following points in mind as you set your goals:

> *A goal is a dream with a deadline!*

- **Visualize your goals.** When you begin to see a dream, you can make it happen. Write your goals down, keeping in mind that a list of goals is more than a list of chores.

- **Make your goals specific.** It's not enough to simply say that you want to be happy, or be successful, or be wealthy, or travel. Your goals also should be measurable; they should have a time frame as well as an intended result. If you don't clearly define these, how will you know when you've reached the goal?

- **Make your goals challenging but realistic.** Set goals you think you can reach: It's better to revise your goals upward than to set them so high that you give up. Setting goals that are unreasonable is self-defeating; they'll only keep you from succeeding.

- **Understand the costs of reaching your goals.** Try to anticipate and plan for the time, money, and effort it will take to get there. Be willing to make some sacrifices, but know how far you are willing to go.

- **Reward yourself when you reach your goals.** Reward yourself for your effort, even if the goal did not turn out completely as expected.

As you think about your business goals, consider a symbol of business prosperity—the frog! The frog is a symbol of business prosperity because it can only move forward. The frog is incapable of moving backward or sideways. And, as one of our students pointed out, sometimes the frog sits still for a very long time, but when the frog moves, it only moves forward.

> *Remember, your goals and business objectives must be in agreement with your basic values.*

To reach your goals, you must make things happen. You are the only one who can build the bridge between imagining your goals and accomplishing them. Self-motivation is the driving force behind high achievement. It's the inner desire that keeps you always moving forward in spite of discouragement, mistakes, and setbacks. There are several steps to self-motivation, including these:

- **Believe in yourself.** Make success and happiness part of your self-image.

- **Think only positive thoughts.** Surround yourself with people who believe in you.

- **Welcome challenges.**

- **Start now.** Don't wait until you have all the information or the circumstances are perfect. Begin now. As your momentum builds, so will your motivation.

- **Focus on the rewards.** Visualize the rewards of success in your mind as clearly and vividly as you can.

- Take pride in your accomplishments.
- Set goals that are stimulating, challenging, and achievable.
- **Start small.** Take control of your day today. This is the first step in achieving success.
- **Once you have a goal, list all of the barriers or obstacles and figure out how you're going to overcome them.**
- **Take control of your fear.** Fear is the opposite of desire. It creates stress, panic, and anxiety and defeats plans and goals. But fear is not all bad because it can slow us down to consider all sides of an issue. To take control of your fear, you must understand where it's coming from. Then take action.
- **Be disciplined.** Being disciplined means sticking to an action plan even when there are other things you'd rather do. It means staying focused and practicing better work habits.
- **Take responsibility for yourself.** Many people are good at blaming others for their own shortcomings. It's easy to blame outside forces for failure. But if you are going to be a successful entrepreneur, you must stop making excuses and take charge of your own life and your own success.
- **Be flexible.** Change is constant; you cannot avoid it. Try to see change as an opportunity instead of as a problem. Change is growth: It can improve your life if you let it.

Practice Writing Effective Goals

Effective goals should be realistic, be measurable, and state a target completion date. Consider the following example:

Goal: Increase sales by $3,000.

Is this goal realistic? Is it measurable? Does it state a target date?

No, it does not have a target date, and we can't tell whether the goal is measurable or realistic because we don't have enough information. Let's change the goal to read:

In 2XXX, sales were $30,000. Increase sales by $3,000 (10 percent) for 2XXY.

See the difference? Now it has a target date and we can determine whether the goal is realistic and measurable.

Read the following statements and rewrite them so they are effective goals:

1. Triple total sales within three months. _____

_____

_____

2. Hire new employees within a year._____

_____

_____

(continued)

(continued)

3. Visit several other businesses to get new ideas. _____

_____

_____

4. Grow from one site to three before Christmas. _____

_____

_____

5. Improve publicity this year. _____

_____

_____

6. Buy a new pickup by the time I start taking jobs. _____

_____

_____

7. Within the next two months, visit community workers who could tell families about my child care service. _____

_____

_____

8. Move work space out of my home. _____

_____

_____

Dana's Day Care, Part I

Dana is a nurse who has always daydreamed about working for herself. She knows she wants to make a living at something she likes to do. She loves working with children, and she has a nice house with a big back yard. Whatever she does, she knows she wants to help people.

Dana spends several months contemplating and researching business ideas before finally deciding to start her own child care business. In May she sets out with a clear, measurable, and realistic goal in mind: *I will open a child care business in my home by September 2XXX with 10 children enrolled.*

Create an Action Plan

An old Chinese proverb applies here: The journey of 10,000 miles starts with a single step. Focusing only on the end result doesn't get you where you need to be today or tomorrow. It only overwhelms you.

You must determine what steps you need to take today to reach your future goal. Planning brings the future into the present so you can do something about it. What must you do to make your dream a reality? What strategy will work best? What resources do you need to get started? As

you create your action plan, consider the amount of money each step will cost you and the amount of time it will take. If you are afraid of taking action, don't look at all the steps ahead of you. Concentrate on one step at a time. Focus just on what is required to complete that single step. Then do it!

An easy way to look at the steps in your action plan is to make a chart with some details for each step. Look at the example for Dana's Day Care that follows.

Dana's Day Care, Part II

Dana has already done some research for her child care business but she knows she needs to write a business plan and prepare her home for the business. She will also need to find her 10 little customers. She starts her Action Plan like this, knowing that she will make changes as she gets more information.

Action	Tasks	Money Requirements	Time Requirements
Write business plan	Take a class or attend a workshop Read books with samples of plans Write plan Have it professionally reviewed	$150.00	8 weeks Complete by June 3rd
Prepare my home for the business	Research the requirements for my home Paint two rooms Purchase toys and other equipment	$500.00	3 hours for 4 weekends Complete by July 13th
Complete the child care paperwork required by my state	Visit the child care office and get a copy of the requirements	$150 for state licenses	5 hours—3 hours to research and 2 hours to complete Complete July 30th
Find 10 customers	Create a short ad for church bulletin Create a flyer to deliver to neighborhood	$5.00—copies	1 hour to create ad 1 hour to create flyer and 2 hours to deliver flyers to neighbors

Three Scenarios

Meet Gail, Jerry, and Daryl. Each has a new business venture. Read the descriptions of their business ideas and the goals they have set for themselves. What do you predict will be the outcome for each? Why?

How to Make an American Quilt

Gail plans to make quilts at home and sell them on consignment through craft boutiques, home decorating stores, and the colonial village tourist site outside of town. She has received a loan of $1,200 to buy a cutting table, cutting tools, and an old sewing machine. Gail's grandmother gave her enough material for at least 25 quilts. Four stores have agreed to take a total of 10 quilts on consignment, and she has a good list of additional stores to contact.

Gail plans to spend about 25 hours a week sewing and 5 hours a week making new contacts. Each quilt takes about 15 hours to make.

Gail has created an action plan with the following goals for the next six months:

- Purchase a table, cutting tools, and supplies within the next two weeks.
- Start sewing by the end of the first month.
- Average 1½ quilts per week and deliver the 10 quilts that have already been accepted for consignment within the first two months.
- Sell eight quilts a month.
- At the end of six months, reevaluate goals and decide whether there is enough business to invite a friend to work with me part time.

Do you think Gail will reach her goals? Are her goals realistic? Are they measurable? Do they state target dates?

_____

_____

Has she listed all of the necessary steps in her action plan?

_____

_____

What changes could she make in her goals and action plan to insure better results?

_____

_____

Painting Himself into a Corner?

Jerry has been painting houses to earn money on the side, helping out a buddy with a painting business. Now Jerry has been laid off from his factory job, and he has decided to start painting full time. His buddy needs help sometimes, but he prefers to work alone when he can handle it, so Jerry has decided to start his own business. Jerry has no experience in soliciting jobs; he has just worked on them.

Jerry can collect unemployment for the first three months, but after his unemployment runs out, he'll have to double his business. To handle that much work, he'll have to hire a helper, which means more expense. So he really needs to *triple* his business to make enough money to cover his bills and living expenses.

Jerry figures that to make it work, he has to meet these goals:

- Get an $8,000 loan to buy a used truck and the ladders and equipment he'll need before he can take any jobs.
- Paint 50 hours a week and do publicity 10 hours a week.
- Find a minimum of three jobs per month for the first three months.
- By the end of three months, increase from three jobs to nine jobs per month and hire a helper.

Are Jerry's goals realistic and measurable?

_____

_____

What are Jerry's chances at success?

_____

_____

What advice would you give to Jerry?

_____

_____

Hot Stuff or a Hot Spot?

Daryl makes a mean chili. His buddies have been telling him for years that he should sell the stuff. He has a job, which he'll keep, but he has decided to start his own business on the side. He's going to call it *Hot Stuff.*

Daryl got the idea for his business while he was at a concert downtown. He saw several food concessions there selling mediocre food at high prices. Daryl figures he has got a better product and can easily make money charging the kind of prices he saw at the concert.

Daryl's got enough money put away to buy a small cart with a warming unit for about $800. He figures the first time there's a big concert downtown, he'll cook up a big batch of his best chili and head for the park. After all, what does he have to lose?

What *does* Daryl have to lose?

_____

_____

What are Daryl's goals?

_____

_____

What additional steps would you include in Daryl's action plan?

_____

_____

Now It's Your Turn

In the exercise that follows, you will state your own goal and outline an action plan to reach it. Be sure to include target dates, the money and time required, and the results. After you write all your goals and action steps, prioritize them and *get started!* Consider asking someone on your support team (see Chapter 2) to review your plan.

My goal is: _____

_____

My Action Plan

Action	Tasks	Money Requirements	Time Requirements
_____	_____	_____	_____
_____	_____	_____	_____
_____	_____	_____	_____
_____	_____	_____	_____
_____	_____	_____	_____
_____	_____	_____	_____
_____	_____	_____	_____
_____	_____	_____	_____
_____	_____	_____	_____
_____	_____	_____	_____

Summing Up

Remember, successful people set goals. Take time to establish goals that will take you where you want to go. Don't forget to create an action plan that lists the tasks and the time and money required to accomplish each. Once you learn how to set goals and create action plans, you can use the same process for any area of your life that you want to change.

In the next chapter, we address a goal that is shared by nearly every entrepreneur as we discuss how to price your products and services to make a profit.

CHAPTER 5

Pricing Your Products and Services

Proper pricing can mean the difference between success and failure in your business. When businesses don't take the time to examine their price structures, they may find (often too late) that they have not priced their products or services properly.

Underpricing can cause a business to fail; if products are drastically underpriced, the business loses money every time a sale is made. Overpricing can cause sales to disappear altogether as customers buy from lower-priced competitors.

In this chapter, you learn about pricing products and services. You also learn how to perform a break-even analysis to determine if your price structure is sound.

Take a minute to consider the implications of pricing products and answer the following questions:

1. Why do you think proper pricing is important?

_____

_____

_____

_____

2. Why do you believe business owners under- or overprice products or services?

_____

_____

_____

_____

_____

3. List some of the consequences of underpricing.

_____

_____

_____

_____

4. Why do you think some business owners are unaware that their products are not properly priced?

_____

_____

_____

_____

_____

A business should have two aims in determining its pricing system: (1) to price its products or services competitively and (2) to ensure that all business expenses can be paid and a profit earned, given a reasonable level of sales. In order to make this happen, the business owner needs to answer the following questions:

- What prices are appropriate for my market?
- What are my business expenses?
- What are reasonable sales goals for my business?

In the following sections, we look at how you can answer each of these questions accurately to ensure proper pricing for your business. But first, lets examine some commonly used pricing strategies.

Pricing Strategies

Businesses use many strategies for pricing their products or services. Not all of these strategies are appropriate for small businesses as some require large amounts of inventory or cash reserves while the business waits for a desired outcome, such as forcing a competitor out of business. Before deciding which pricing tactic to use in your small business, consider the time and money it will take to make each strategy successful and the possible risks involved.

- **Promotional pricing:** In this common strategy, businesses promote specific products or lines at a reduced price in order to generate interest, launch a new product, or sell in quantity. Examples of promotional pricing include a Summer Dress Sale, a President's Day Sale, or a Buy One Get One Free deal. This temporary strategy is appropriate for most retail businesses at some point in time.

- **Close out pricing:** An example of this strategy is when businesses offer lower prices to try to sell off unwanted stock, excess inventory, out-of-season items, or perishable items that are near their expiration date. This way the business avoids the expense of having to store or discard the merchandise and lures customers in with the promise of bargains.

- **Quantity pricing:** Also called *multiple unit pricing,* this involves offering a lower price to customers who purchase multiple units or large quantities of products or services. This can generate additional sales and attract customers who are in the market to place large orders. Business owners should be careful not to discount so heavily that they are pricing items below cost, however.

- **Product line or version pricing:** This is when a business sells a range of products at varying prices based on varying benefits. For example, a business may sell a basic car wash for $5, but also sell $7, $9, and $12 car washes that include additional benefits, such as added wheel cleaner, hot wax, and hand drying. This can be an effective way to increase sales while offering attractive benefits to customers.

- **Bundling:** This is when a business sells individual items bundled together at a price that is lower than if the customer purchased each item seperately. By bundling a hot seller with lesser-known or slow-moving items, businesses can increase sales and move hard-to-sell inventory at the same time. Electronic items such as cameras, video games, and computers are commonly offered in bundles.

- **Psychological pricing:** This is when businesses price their products in a way that is psychologically attractive to customers. For example, pricing an item at $9.99 instead of $10, or selling a product for $39.99 and advertising it as "All for under $40!" This plays to the emotional rather than the rational side of the buyer.

- **Captive product pricing:** This is a strategy where an initial product is sold at a low price, but requires the purchase of high-priced complementary sales in order for the buyer to use or continue using the product. Examples include razors that are inexpensive but require pricey, one-of-a-kind blade refills, or software packages (such as virus protection) with low introductory prices that require expensive annual upgrades.

- **Loss leader pricing:** This strategy is often used in grocery stores where a product is temporarily advertised at a sale price below the store's cost. The grocery store owner knows he will lose money each time a customer buys that $1.99 gallon of milk, but the objective is to get customers into the store and tempt them into buying more items while they're there. They often position the loss leader item at the back of the store, forcing the customer to walk past many potential purchases on the way in and out of the store.

- **Destroyer pricing:** Here, a company charges a price below average in an attempt to drive the competition out of business. Again, this strategy is not appropriate for most small businesses because their financial resources aren't sufficient to achieve this goal.

- **Price skimming:** This temporary strategy is often used when a new, innovative product is first introduced. In the beginning, high prices can be charged because the product is unique and in high demand; there are usually no competitors during this initial period. Once the newness of the product wears off or competitors start to offer similar products, the price comes down. This is often seen when high-tech electronic items first hit the market—for example, DVD players and High Definition televisions. Price skimming is also used when a situation creates an unusual demand for a product (think of trying to buy a snow shovel during a snow storm). Customers may pay the higher price when they have no other choice, but in the long term, this is a risky strategy as customers may feel taken advantage of and refuse to buy from the business in the future.

- **Price discrimination:** When businesses charge different people different prices for effectively the same product, they are using price discrimination. Airlines and hotels use this strategy often; you'll seldom find two people on a flight who paid the same price for their seat. The business may quote a price based on factors such as when the customer buys the service in relationship to when they will use it, what other events are occurring at the time the service will be used, or what discounts the customer may be entitled to. In reality, businesses that use this strategy are trying to charge each customer the maximum amount he or she is willing to pay. While this is an accepted practice in some industries, it is not tolerated in others (imagine paying more for a cheeseburger because you went through the drive-thru as opposed to going inside to order).

What Price Is Right?

While each of the strategies outlined previously can be useful for a particular business or in a particular situation, the real price of a product or service is simply no more than the customer is willing to pay. Finding that out requires some research. Below are several sources of information on pricing. Use as many of them as you can to determine what prices are appropriate for your market.

Customer Surveys

One way to determine pricing is to survey your potential customers. This is possible only if you can identify and locate your potential customers, which is difficult for some businesses. It also may be a challenge to get an honest answer to the question, "How much would you be willing to pay for this?" Some businesses mail surveys to their target customers, and some survey individuals in public places.

Shopping Your Competition

Another way to find out what the market will bear is to "shop" the competition. If your competitors operate from retail stores, a quick trip to their shops allows you to see what they charge for similar products and services and whether they appear to be making sales. You can make phone calls to determine hourly rates commonly charged by service industry competitors. This way, you not only find out what your competitors charge, but you also get a good feel for their level of customer service—for example, whether they are respectful to their customers, answer and return phone calls promptly, and are knowledgeable about their industry.

Market Research Sales

Selling your goods or services at a marketplace or fair—or temporarily subleasing a small space in an existing shop—is an effective way to determine appropriate pricing, as well as help you determine whether your business idea is feasible. This approach also gives you hands-on experience at operating your business. In order to use this approach, you will need a small supply of inventory. You should make certain you are not required to rent booth or floor space in a long-term lease. Remember, this is just an exercise in market research to help you determine how to price your products.

While you operate your temporary business, listen to what your customers tell you. If customers continually comment on how low your prices are, you may have some room to raise them. On the other hand, if your products create interest but no sales, you might consider lowering your prices.

What Are Your Expenses?

In order to operate a successful business, the pricing structure must take into account all of the expenses of running the business. Expenses must be identified and divided into two categories: cost of goods sold (also call *variable* or *direct expenses*) and fixed expenses (also call *overhead* or *indirect expenses*).

Cost of Goods Sold

The direct expenses of creating your product or service are called the *cost of goods sold* (COGS). If your business sells wooden toys that are handcrafted and painted, then the wood, the paint, and the time it takes to make the toys are all COGS. If your business sells beaded jewelry, then all of the materials (beads, thread, glue, clasps, pins, etc.) plus the cost of labor (the time it takes to make each piece of jewelry) are the COGS. If you provide a service, such as a secretarial service, the COGS might include paper and file folders plus the cost of the labor. In a cleaning business, the COGS might include cleaning supplies, transportation costs for cleaning crews, and labor. COGS are sometimes referred to as *variable expenses* because they "vary" (go up and down) in relationship to sales. The more widgets your business sells, the higher the total cost to make those widgets; the fewer widgets sold, the fewer widget production costs you'll have.

Fixed Expenses

Some expenses exist whether or not a business has any sales. These are called *fixed expenses.* Examples of typical fixed expenses include rent, insurance, utilities, legal and accounting costs, and advertising. Fixed expenses are usually recurring expenses for things that are consumed (or used up) during the course of normal operations. These expenses sometimes are referred to as *overhead expenses.* Fixed expenses do not substantially increase or decrease with changes in sales volume. Because of this, fixed expenses are easy to identify and predict.

Capital Expenditures

There is a third type of expense: *capital expenditures.* Capital expenditures include the cost of purchasing nonrecurring major items for your business that are not consumed (used up) during normal business operations—for example, one-time purchases of land, buildings, furniture, or major equipment. Capital expenditures usually exceed a certain dollar amount (which varies from business to business) and increase the value of your business (your business is worth more if you sell it). Capital expenditures are not included in the break-even calculation or considered when pricing products. New business owners include capital expenditures in their start-up costs, however. As a business grows or equipment needs to be replaced, additional capital expenditures are paid for out of net profit.

The Break-Even Analysis

After you identify your COGS and your fixed expenses, you can perform a *break-even analysis.* This tells you how many products or services you must sell at a given price in order to cover the expenses of your business. The *break-even point* is the point at which adequate sales are made to cover your business expenses, but before a profit is earned. It's important to perform this analysis because it allows you to determine whether your price structure is sound. It will also set minimal sales goals for your business.

Before we actually perform a break-even analysis, we need to define a few terms:

- **Gross income** is the amount of income a business earns before expenses are considered.
- **Gross profit** is what remains when you subtract the cost of goods sold from the gross income. Fixed expenses are paid from the gross profit.
- **Net profit** is what remains when you subtract the fixed expenses from the gross profit.

The box on the right shows you how this information is typically put together.

When Will You Break Even?

In order for your business to survive, you must have sufficient gross income so that there is enough gross profit to pay all of your fixed expenses after you subtract your cost of goods sold. The break-even point defines the actual number of products or services you must sell at a certain price in order to achieve this. A new business performs a break-even analysis after assuming the following three things:

1. **Gross income (or price) per product or service:** At first, this number is an educated guess based on what you learned about the marketplace. The break-even analysis will confirm whether or not this price is sufficient.

2. **Cost of goods sold per product or service:** You find this number by researching the cost of creating the product or service.

3. **Fixed expenses of the business:** This information comes from researching the cost of operating the business.

ABC Widgets & Gadgets

Income

Sales/Widgets	$500.00
Sales/Gadgets	+$400.00
Gross Income	*$900.00*

Cost of Goods Sold

Materials	$250.00
Labor	+$350.00
Total COGS	*$600.00*
Gross Profit	*$300.00*

Fixed Expenses

Rent	$100.00
Utilities	+$35.00
Owner's compensation	+$100.00
Total Fixed Expenses	*$235.00*
Net Profit	***$65.00***

After you gather this information, you can perform a break-even analysis using the following two-part formula:

Gross income − cost of goods sold = gross profit

Fixed expenses ÷ gross profit = break-even point

For example, if we assume the following about a widget business:

Gross income per widget =	$9
Cost of goods sold per widget =	$4
Fixed expenses per month =	$1,000

then we can perform the break-even analysis as follows:

Gross income	$9
− cost of goods sold	− $4
= gross profit	$5
Fixed expenses	$1,000
÷ gross profit	÷ $5
= break-even point	200

This business must sell 200 widgets per month at $9 per widget to break even.

Now go through the following example to see how Sarah Sue performs a break-even analysis for her new business.

Sarah Sue's Scenario

All of Sarah Sue's friends rave about her sandwiches (she makes them with her secret sandwich sauce). With a great deal of encouragement from her family and friends, Sarah Sue is thinking about opening her own sandwich shop. At this point, she is in the information-gathering stage.

Sarah Sue has learned that a local deli owner is about to retire, and she has talked with him about renting his storefront. (This will cost her $600 per month.) Sarah Sue also got information about the costs of utilities for the storefront (about $150 per month), telephone (about $100 per month), and business insurance ($25 per month). Sarah Sue examined her personal situation and made a determination about how much money she needs to earn in order to meet her financial obligations ($2,000 per month).

Armed with this information, Sarah Sue came up a list of fixed expenses for Sarah Sue's Sandwich Shop (see sidebar).

Next, Sarah Sue must calculate the cost of goods sold for her sandwiches. Since the ingredients for the sandwiches will vary by order, Sarah Sue decides to start with what she believes will be her most popular sandwich: turkey and Swiss cheese on whole wheat (known as the Swiss Gobbler). She calculates the cost of making this sandwich with everything on it, as this will represent the highest COGS. Having received a price sheet from her food supplier, Sarah Sue came up with these figures:

Fixed Expenses

Rent	$600
Utilities	$150
Telephone	$100
Business insurance	$25
Owner's compensation	$2,000
Miscellaneous	$50
Total fixed expenses:	$2,925

Supplier Price Sheet and Labor Costs	Sarah Estimates	Ingredients per Swiss Gobbler	COGS Swiss Gobbler
Turkey $3.00/lb.	10 slices/lb.	2 slices	$.60
Bread $.75/loaf	30 slices/loaf	2 slices	$.05
Swiss cheese $3.00/lb.	10 slices/lb.	2 slices	$.60
Mayonnaise $2.00/jar	32 ounces/jar	1 ounce	$.06
Mustard $1.00/jar	32 ounces/jar	1 ounce	$.03
Tomatoes $.50 ea.	8 slices/tomato	2 slices	$.13
Lettuce $.60/head	30 leaves/head	2 leaves	$.04
Secret sauce $3.00/jar	32 ounces/jar	1 ounce	$.09
Wax paper $.03/sheet	precut sheets	1 sheet	$.03
Labor $8.00/hr.	20 sandwiches/hr.	3 minutes	$.40
Total COGS:			**$2.03**

Sarah Sue has determined that it will cost her $2.03 to create her most popular sandwich. She has shopped the competition and surveyed her friends, and she believes that a fair price for this sandwich will be $4.95. Given these assumptions, Sarah Sue calculates the following:

> Gross income − COGS = gross profit
>
> $4.95 − $2.03 = $2.92
>
> Fixed expenses ÷ gross profit = break-even point
>
> $2,925 ÷ $2.92 = 1,001

Sarah Sue will have to sell 1,001 Swiss Gobblers (or similarly priced sandwiches) each month to break even. To break the calculation down further, if Sarah Sue is open for business 6 days a week, or about 25 days each month, she will need to sell about 40 sandwiches per day to break even.

> 1,001 sandwiches ÷ 25 days a month = 40.04 sandwiches a day

Now she can ask herself whether this seems like a reasonable goal.

Henri's Hemp Tote Bags

Henriette sells 100% organic hemp market tote bags from her Web site. She offers bags in three basic colors, each with a choice of contrasting colored handles. Some of her bags have outside pockets, but all are the same basic size and shape. She manufactures her bags from home and mails them to customers all over the country.

Henri sells her bags for $30 each plus $5 shipping and handling.

Her material costs average $7 per bag. She pays herself $12 per hour to make the bags and she can produce 3 bags per hour. On average, it costs her $4 to package and mail a bag.

Henri's monthly fixed expenses include

- High speed Internet service: $50
- Telephone: $60
- Office supplies: $50
- Bookkeeping service: $80
- Owner's compensation: $1,500

Use the following worksheets to calculate Henri's break-even point. You can use Worksheet 2 at the end of this chapter to calculate break-even points for businesses selling one major product (including your own).

Henri's Fixed Expenses

Rent _____

Utilities _____

Telephone _____

Office supplies _____

Internet service _____

Insurance _____

Professional fees _____

Owner's compensation _____

Total Monthly Fixed Expenses: _____

Worksheet: Pricing/Break-Even Analysis for Individual Products

Product Name: Henri's Hemp Tote Bags

Part 1

Gross Income	–	COGS	=	Gross Profit

Part 2

Fixed Expenses	÷	Gross Profit	=	Break-Even Point

Selling Multiple Products

Most businesses sell more than one product at varied prices. Follow these four steps to calculate the break-even point for a business selling multiple products:

1. Start by determining the average gross profit margin on each of the products sold.

   - Begin by defining the products by categories (A). For example, let's say a T-shirt shop sells primarily three types or categories of products: T-shirts, sweatshirts, and hats.

   - Next, calculate the Average Selling Price (B) and Average Cost (C) for each category. In this example, T-shirts sell for an average price of $15 and their cost is around $7. Sweatshirts sell for about $25 and cost roughly $15. Hats sell for about $9 and cost $5.

- Calculate the Gross Profit (D) (selling price minus cost) per category.

- Determine the Gross Profit Margin (E) of each category. Show this as a percent. This is done by taking gross profit and dividing it by the selling price. The following table shows these calculations:

A. Product Category	B. Average Selling Price	C. Average Cost	D. Gross Profit (selling price – cost)	E. Gross Profit Margin (gross profit / selling price)
T-Shirts	$15	$7	$15 –$7 = $8	$8 / $15 = .53 or 53%
Sweatshirts	$25	$15	$25 – $15 = $10	$10 / $25 = .40 or 40%
Hats	$9	$5	$9 – $5 = $4	$4 / $9 = .44 or 44%

2. Once this has been done for each category, come up with an Average Gross Profit Margin (average the three selling prices; average the three gross profit amounts; then divide the average gross profit by the average selling price). The average gross profit margin for this T-shirt business is 44%.

Average Selling Prices	Average Gross Profit	Average Gross Profit Margin
($15+$25+$9) / 3 = $16	($8+$10+$4) / 3 = $7	$7 / $16 = .44 or 44%

3. The next step is to determine the average monthly fixed expenses. Following are the monthly fixed expenses for this business:

Average Monthly Fixed Expenses

Rent	$500
Insurance	$100
Utilities	$200
Owner's salary	$1,000
Telephone	$70
Marketing	$130
Misc.	$100
Total Fixed Expenses	$2,100

4. The final step in determining the break-even point is to apply this formula:

Fixed expenses ÷ gross profit margin = breakeven sales

$2,100 ÷ .44 = $4,772

This business must sell $4,772 worth of products each month to breakeven. Notice that this break-even point doesn't tell the business owner how many T-shirts, sweatshirts, and hats she must sell to break even. Instead, calculating breakeven this way tells the owner how much total monthly sales she must generate in order to reach her monthly break-even point.

As before, the business owner can divide this number by the number of days he is open for business and arrive at his daily break-even point. Assuming this T-shirt business is open 26 days per month, the owner's daily break-even sales goal is ($4,772 divided by 26) $185.54.

Mary's Lions, Tigers, and Bears

Mary is an artisan who makes unique creations from a studio in her home. She makes one-of–a-kind stuffed animals in three sizes: small (babies), large (adult animals), and giant (such as 6-foot-tall giraffes). Her COGS can be calculated as follows:

- Mary sells her small stuffed animals for $35. Her materials costs average $5, and the small animals take Mary about 1 hour to make. She calculates her production labor at $10 per hour; therefore, her total cost to produce one small animal is: $_____.

- Large animals sell for $70. Materials costs average $18 and they take about 1.5 hours to make; therefore, her total cost to produce one large animal is: $ _____.

- The giant animals sell for $150. Materials costs are typically $35. Mary spends about 4 hours making a giant animal. This makes her total cost to produce a giant animal: $_____.

Following are Mary's fixed expenses:

- A friend of Mary's has a shop in the village that sells hand-painted children's furniture and bedding. She has agreed to display Mary's stuffed animals in one corner of her shop for a flat fee of $300 per month.

- Mary also has a business phone line for which she pays $75 per month.

- She would like to be able to draw an owner's salary of $1,000 per month.

Based on this information, use Worksheet 1 to calculate Mary's fixed expenses, and Worksheet 3 to calculate her monthly break-even sales point. Then answer the following questions:

1. Which of Mary's products has the highest gross profit margin?

2. What is Mary's monthly break-even sales point?

3. Do you think Mary's business idea is viable? Why or why not?

Owner's Compensation

What is the most common mistake small business owners make? Thinking their own labor is "free." If a business owner fails to include the cost of his or her time when calculating prices, the income will never be there to pay the owner. Smart business owners include the cost of their time in two places: in fixed expenses as a salary (this pays the owner for the administrative time it takes to *manage* the business) and in Cost of Goods Sold as an hourly wage (so the owner gets paid for the time spent *producing products*). Until sales reach the break-even point, you may choose not to take your salary or hourly wage out of the business, but at least it will be built into your pricing structure.

Worksheet #1: Fixed Expenses

When identifying your monthly fixed expenses, use the average of what you expect your monthly expenses to be in the first six months. Include your target amount for owner's compensation. If you do not include your compensation in your pricing structure, you might find yourself working for free.

Fixed Expenses

Rent   _____

Utilities   _____

Telephone   _____

Office supplies   _____

Postage   _____

Equipment repairs & maintenance   _____

Insurance   _____

Loan payments   _____

Marketing costs   _____

Subscriptions/Dues/Fees   _____

Legal/Accounting   _____

Owner's compensation   _____

Other _____   _____

_____   _____

_____   _____

_____   _____

Total Monthly Fixed Expenses: _____

Worksheet #1: Fixed Expenses

You can use this copy of the worksheet to calculate the fixed expenses for your own business.

When identifying your monthly fixed expenses, use the average of what you expect your monthly expenses to be in the first six months. Include your target amount for owner's compensation. If you do not include your compensation in your pricing structure, you will never be able to afford to pay yourself this amount.

Fixed Expenses

Rent   _____

Utilities   _____

Telephone   _____

Office supplies   _____

Postage   _____

Equipment repairs & maintenance   _____

Insurance   _____

Loan payments   _____

Marketing costs   _____

Subscriptions/Dues/Fees   _____

Legal/Accounting   _____

Owner's compensation   _____

Other _____   _____

_____   _____

_____   _____

_____   _____

Total Monthly Fixed Expenses: _____

Worksheet #2: Pricing/Break-Even Analysis

You can use this worksheet to practice calculating the break-even point for each of Mary's individual products.

Individual Products

Product Name: _____

Part 1

Gross Income	–	COGS	=	Gross Profit

Part 2

Fixed Expenses	÷	Gross Profit	=	Break-Even Point

Product Name: _____

Part 1

Gross Income	–	COGS	=	Gross Profit

Part 2

Fixed Expenses	÷	Gross Profit	=	Break-Even Point

Product Name: _____

Part 1

Gross Income	–	COGS	=	Gross Profit

Part 2

Fixed Expenses	÷	Gross Profit	=	Break-Even Point

Worksheet #2: Pricing/Break-Even Analysis

You can use this copy of the worksheet to calculate the break-even for your own products.

Individual Products

Product Name: _____

Part 1

Gross Income	–	COGS	=	Gross Profit

Part 2

Fixed Expenses	÷	Gross Profit	=	Break-Even Point

Product Name: _____

Part 1

Gross Income	–	COGS	=	Gross Profit

Part 2

Fixed Expenses	÷	Gross Profit	=	Break-Even Point

Product Name: _____

Part 1

Gross Income	–	COGS	=	Gross Profit

Part 2

Fixed Expenses	÷	Gross Profit	=	Break-Even Point

Worksheet #3: Pricing/Break-Even Analysis for Multiple Products

Part 1

A. Product Category	B. Average Selling Price	C. Average Cost	D. Gross Profit (selling price – cost)	E. Gross Profit Margin (gross profit / selling price)
Category 1				
Category 2				
Category 3				
Category 4				
Category 5				
Overall Averages				

Part 2

Monthly Fixed Expenses ÷ by Gross Profit Margin = Monthly Break-Even Sales		

Worksheet #3: Pricing/Break-Even Analysis for Multiple Products

You can use this copy of the worksheet to calculate the monthly break-even point for your own business.

A. Product Category	B. Average Selling Price	C. Average Cost	D. Gross Profit (selling price – cost)	E. Gross Profit Margin (gross profit / selling price)
Category 1				
Category 2				
Category 3				
Category 4				
Category 5				
Overall Averages				

Part 2

Monthly Fixed Expenses ÷ by Gross Profit Margin = Monthly Break-Even Sales		

Pricing for Service Providers

Not everyone sells a product. Some small businesses sell their time and know-how to clients who need professional services. Service providers include therapists, accountants, consultants, designers, technicians, writers, and other small businesses that primarily sell their time and expertise.

This formula (and the worksheet on page 61) can be used to determine an appropriate hourly billing rate for a service provider:

Step 1. Determine your income requirements. Estimate your annual operating expenses (sometimes called overhead). These should include things such as rent, utilities, insurance, and telephone service.

Next, decide how much personal income you need to earn. Don't forget to include the cost of self-employment tax, your estimated federal tax liability, and the cost of health insurance premiums.

Annual operating expenses:	$10,000
Owner's gross wages:	$30,000
Total income requirements:	$40,000

Step 2. Calculate available working hours. Multiply the number of weeks per year by the number of work hours per week.

52 weeks x 40 hours per week: 2,080 total hours

Subtract time off for annual vacations and holidays to get your total available work hours per year.

− 40 vacation hours and 56 holiday hours: 2,080 − 96 = 1,984 available hours

Step 3. Estimate billable hours. Estimate what percentage of your available time you will be able to bill clients. Consider your expectations for gaining new jobs or new clients over time. This percentage may have seasonal fluctuations, depending on your business. Break down these estimates by months or quarters.

1,984 hours available per year

1,984 ÷ 4 quarters = 496 hours available per quarter

	Available Hours	x	Percentage Billable Hours	=	Billable Hours per Quarter
Quarter 1:	496	x	20% (1 day per week)		99
Quarter 2:	496	x	25% (1 out of 4 days)		124
Quarter 3:	496	x	30% (1 out of 3 days)		149
Quarter 4:	496	x	40% (2 days per week)		198
Estimated Billable Hours:					570

Step 4. Calculate your hourly billing rate. Divide your total required income (from Step 1) by the number of estimated billable hours per year (from Step 3) to get your hourly rate.

$$\$40,000 \div 570 \text{ hours} = \$70.18 \text{ per hour}$$

Step 5. Evaluate. Does the rate seem reasonable? Consider what the market will bear. Your answer depends on the type of service you provide and your competition. If the rate is not reasonable, how can you adjust it? Is your salary goal too high? Can you reduce overhead expenses or increase billable hours? Can you accomplish this amount of work and manage your business while maintaining a reasonable schedule? Is this a viable business, given your financial and lifestyle goals?

Summing Up

Now that you have finished the exercises in this chapter and completed your analysis, ask yourself the following questions:

- **Does your pricing seem reasonable?** Consider what the market will bear. The answer depends on the products you are providing and your competition.

- **If your prices are not reasonable, can you adjust them?** Can you minimize your cost of goods sold without sacrificing quality? Is your owner's compensation goal too high? Are there fixed expenses that can be reduced or eliminated? If your expenses cannot be reduced substantially, can your estimated sales be reasonably increased?

- **Are your sales goals reasonable?** Take into account your local competition. Also take into account your business hours. Are your sales estimates reasonable for the number of hours your business will be open?

- **If you will be providing the bulk of the labor, how many hours will it take for you to meet your production goals?** In the example of Mary's business, she may determine that she will have to work more hours for less personal income to be self-employed. If this is the case for you, ask yourself if that is consistent with your financial and lifestyle goals. Can you accomplish this amount of work and manage your business while maintaining a reasonable schedule?

The answers to these questions will help you decide whether your business idea is viable.

Once you've made the commitment to start your business, track your actual expenses and sales. Compare your actual numbers to your original estimates. Review these numbers often and adjust your estimates accordingly. The longer your business operates, the more information you will have and the better your estimates will become.

Service Providers/Hourly Rate Worksheet

Annual Operating Expenses

Rent		_____
Utilities	+	_____
Telephone	+	_____
Office supplies	+	_____
Postage	+	_____
Equipment repairs & maintenance	+	_____
Business insurance	+	_____
Loan payments	+	_____
Marketing costs	+	_____
Subscriptions/Dues/Fees	+	_____
Legal/Accounting	+	_____
Travel & entertainment	+	_____
Other _____	+	_____
_____		_____
_____		_____
_____		_____
_____		_____
Total annual operating expenses:	=	_____
Owner's annual compensation:	+	_____
Self-employment taxes:	+	_____
Annual health insurance cost:	+	_____
#1. Total income required:	=	_____

Total working hours per year
(52 weeks x 40 hours)   2,080

Less vacation hours: – _____

Less holiday hours: – _____

#2. Available working hours per year   = _____

Available working hours per quarter
(available hours per year ÷ 4)   = _____

Estimated Billable Hours per Quarter

	Available Hours per Quarter		Percent Billable Hours		Billable Hours per Quarter
Quarter 1:	_____	x	_____	=	_____
Quarter 2:	_____	x	_____	=	_____
Quarter 3:	_____	x	_____	=	_____
Quarter 4:	_____	x	_____	=	_____

#3. Estimated billable hours per year: = _____

#4. Total income required ÷ **total billable hours per year** = **hourly rate:** = _____

#5. Is this reasonable? _____

CHAPTER 6

Reaching Your Customers

Many people dream of starting a business so they can make a living doing work that they enjoy and excel at. But when you are just starting out, you'll find that you spend most of your time trying to find people who will pay you for your work. Although you are good at your chosen occupation, you may be uncomfortable when it comes to marketing your business. Yet marketing is one of the most important things you will do, not only as you start but also as you continue to run your business.

When you hear the word *marketing,* you may think of advertising, promotions, public relations, or market research. Indeed, marketing includes all of these. It sounds complicated and expensive, and some marketing departments in large corporations do have enormous budgets. But you can make your marketing efforts fun and inexpensive. Just remember, you can only *sell* your product or service to your customers if they *know* about your product or service.

Marketing means making potential customers aware of your product or service and getting them to try it for the very first time. In this chapter we show you how.

The Five Marketing Questions

Before you spend any money on marketing, take the time to research and consider the following questions. When you are educated about your product or service and understand your customers, you are ready to make decisions about the best ways to reach them.

1. What is your product or service?

2. Who are your potential customers?

3. How do you reach your customers?

4. What other businesses are offering the same product or service?

5. How will you deliver your product or service to keep customers coming back for more?

What Is Your Product or Service?

The first step in developing a marketing plan is to be very clear about what you are selling. You must be able to describe your product or service in precise terms that anyone can understand. Before you can sell your product or service to a potential customer, you must also be convinced that what you offer is terrific. After all, if *you* don't believe in what you are selling, no one will. On the next page are some questions to start you thinking about the best way to describe your product or service.

● What product or service do you provide? Don't forget to include support services you offer (for example, delivery, maintenance, or house calls).

_____

_____

● What makes your product or service special? How is your product or service different from ones that are already on the market? _____

_____

_____

● Why will people want to buy your product or service? _____

_____

_____

● Add any other information about your product or service you think is important.

_____

_____

Is there *both* a *market* and a *need* for your product or service? Sometimes there is a need for a product or service but there are not enough people to purchase it to maintain a business. In that case, there is a need but not a market. For example, there is a need for more low income housing, but is there a paying market to rent or buy the properties? Later in this chapter we will discuss how to determine whether there are enough potential customers so you can determine whether you can make your business profitable.

One of the biggest mistakes beginning entrepreneurs make is not having a clear product or service to sell. They try to sell something to everyone. Their message gets lost and they confuse the consumer. As your business grows, you may be able to expand your services and products, but in the beginning, it's crucial to focus, focus, focus!

Below are examples of entrepreneurs and their products and services. Read through the examples and decide who is **ready** to market to their potential customers (**R**), who is too **narrowly** focused (**N**), and who needs to **focus** their product or service more (**F**). Circle your response.

A florist who does not provide a delivery service. R   N   F

A small clothing store that offers punk styles, business outfits, maternity clothes, and formal dresses. R   N   F

A seamstress who sews new clothes and does alterations for middle-income women. She will make house calls or do fittings at her workshop by appointment. R   N   F

A hairdresser who works alone, trying to develop a walk-in business and do home visits at the same time. R   N   F

A caterer with excellent home-cooked food who puts care into arranging beautiful table displays. She does not provide servers, but has a list of people she can recommend. R   N   F

An upholsterer who does sewing and refinishing but expects customers to bring their own material. R   N   F

An experienced daycare provider who offers educational toys, snacks, a play area, and flexible hours. R   N   F

A delivery service that promises next-day delivery but does not pick up after noon. R   N   F

A single person doing roofing, indoor/outdoor painting, carpentry, and household repairs. R   N   F

A landscaper offering landscape design, a 15-percent discount arrangement with the local garden center, delivery, installation, and maintenance. R   N   F

A house painter emphasizing quality work but using a cheap grade of paint to save customers money. R   N   F

Who Are Your Potential Customers?

The second question to answer is who are your customers and what do they want. Once you know your customers, you can begin to develop a plan to reach them. You have limited time and money, so it's important to target your resources to people who are most likely to buy from you.

The answer to this question is *not* "everyone." Define your customers by narrowing down characteristics until you find your target market. Example: A daycare provider who is going to start her business in her home can assume the following about her customers: They live relatively close by. They have children. They are mostly working parents. They make enough money to afford childcare. As you can see, the "everyone" answer quickly becomes more manageable and more targetable. Once our daycare provider determines the characteristics of her customers, she can begin to reach out to them.

When you think of your product or service, what common characteristics do you think your potential customers might have? If your customers will be organizations or businesses, what characteristics will they have in common?

The following worksheet can help you get started. When you are finished, go back and **circle** the characteristics that will help you define your customers best.

> ***Make sure you offer only what your market wants to buy.***

Customers

Individual Customers

Income level _____	Job and position _____
Sex, age, marital status _____	Religion _____
Education _____	Location _____
Health _____	Hobbies, skills _____
Race _____	Number of children _____
Own or rent a home _____	Age and type of car _____

(continued)

(continued)

Vacation activities _____	Household pets _____
Eating habits _____	Spending habits _____

Organizations

Vacation activities _____	Household pets _____
Industry _____	Size _____
Profit/Not-for-profit _____	Number of employees _____
Location _____	

Now further define your potential customers. If you circled income level, what income will your potential customers most likely have? Read the following example and then write your own customer description.

Sara is a Yoga teacher and wants to start her own Yoga studio. Her customer description might read like this: "My typical customer is a woman, aged 45–60, with average income and a desire to be healthy." That doesn't mean that Sara won't have some customers who are male or wealthy or younger. But Sara believes her *typical* customers will fit the above description. Sara can use her description to help her research the potential market. When she begins to advertise, she can go back to her description to decide the best way for her to reach her target customers.

Write a description of your potential customers in the space below:

_____

_____

_____

Now that you have a description of your potential customers, it's time to research how many people fit your description.

Research the Market

You want to gather as much information about your potential customers as possible so that you can prove there is a market for your product or service. As you do this research, you may become convinced that your business idea is viable, or you may discover that the number of people who would buy your product or service is not large enough and you should explore other possibilities.

One place to start is demographic reports. *Demographics* refers to selected population characteristics such as race, age, income, disabilities, educational attainment, home ownership, and employment status. You can find this demographic information on federal government and city, county, and state Web sites. You may also find valuable information in industry surveys and statistics.

Be sure to evaluate the quality of your sources and the timing of the information. If you are using industry statistics, are they over-reaching to prove there is a market? If you're using census data, when was the data compiled? Census data is collected every 10 years and takes a couple of years to produce. In some cases, it won't make a difference. But, if you are in an area that is experiencing great change, take that into consideration as you research your potential market.

Use the data you gather to estimate the number of customers you can expect. Answer the question: Are there enough people who fit my customer description to support my business? Then use your research to predict the potential for growth in your business. Will the number of customers increase or decrease? Look at the product or service that you are offering. Read trade articles and talk with people already in the industry to determine if the industry is growing or losing ground.

Gathering your resources and using the information to make your case can be fun. You won't come up with absolutes, but you will know much more about your customer base and have more confidence in your business idea.

There are several sources of information on the business community and customer base in your area. Check these out first; then brainstorm with your support team to come up with other possibilities.

- **The Internet:** Many sites can provide you with information about your potential market. A good place to begin your search is the U.S. Census Bureau site at http://factfinder.census.gov.

- **The public library:** Here you can get information on the size and makeup of your market, the number of people per household, family income, the number of home-owners and home values, and the number of cars per household. This kind of information is available for both the national and local levels, so you can compare the two. Here are some of the information sources you will find at your local library:

  - *Encyclopedia of Associations:* Lists trade associations, including addresses and phone numbers and a list of publications.

  - *Measuring Markets:* A Guide to the Use of Federal and State Statistical Data will help you find specific publications with market information for the geographic area that interests you.

  - *Census of Population and Housing, Standard Metropolitan Statistical Areas, and Census Tract Reports.*

  - *County Business Patterns:* Summarizes information on businesses by state and county. Information is provided by business type, number and size of businesses, and number of employees.

  - *Reference USA:* A database for your community. You will quickly learn about your competitors. Ask your librarian if they have a copy of *Reference USA* or go to http://www.referenceusa.com/.

- **The Yellow Pages.**
- **Competitors:** Check out your competition's marketing literature, Web sites, and publicity; observe how customers are treated; look at the same type of business in another community or town.
- **Wholesalers and manufacturers.**
- **Federal and state governments.**
- **Business, trade, and professional journals and meetings.**

- Chambers of commerce and local governments.
- Community development corporations.
- **Potential customers:** Watch your potential customers in action and interview or survey them.

Now that you've identified who your potential customers are, take a look at what might be important to them.

What Are Your Customers Looking For?

Below is a list of qualities customers look for in products and services. Scan through them and then list in the spaces provided the three qualities you think are the most important to customers who would buy your product or service.

• Durability	• Style	• Cost
• Variety	• Promptness	• Reliability
• Ease of care	• Efficiency	• Comfort
• Craftsmanship	• Quality	• Innovation

1. _____

2. _____

3. _____

How Do You Reach Your Customers?

So now you've defined your product or service and you have an idea of who your customers will be and what is important to them. In this section, we look at several ways to make those potential customers aware of your product or service. Certain ideas will work better for some businesses than for others. However, every entrepreneur should remember one overarching idea: Business is about relationships!

In your personal life, you don't meet a person, spend a few minutes with him or her, and immediately become best friends. It's the same in business: It takes time for potential customers to understand and trust you and your product or service. As you spread the word about your business, you will meet lots of people who are interested in it but who don't need or want to buy from you at that time. Consider and work with these people as potential customers. They are an investment for the future of your business.

Here are some simple ways to make your potential customers aware of your product or service and to encourage them to buy from you. Keep your profile of potential customers in mind as you consider these ideas.

Create a Brand

Earlier, we discussed the importance of a good name for your business. But there is more to creating a brand than a name. Should you also consider a logo? What written materials will you need? Business cards? Stationery? Brochures? Every piece of written material should incorporate your business brand whether it's a logo or just the special font you use for your name. Also be sure everything you produce is easy to read and gives the potential customer basic information about your business. You can use software programs to create a professional image for all of your written materials. Consider Microsoft Publisher or FrontPage or Adobe Photoshop.

Your business brand comes across strongly on the phone as well. Think about how you will answer the phone and consider the impression you want to give. If you have employees who answer the phones, you must take time to explain to them the image you are trying to create.

Regardless of your specific brand, be sure that everything about your business also reflects that *you are a professional.* Many businesses today are located in private homes, and customers either don't know or don't care. However, if your business is located in your home and you are worried that customers might view this as unprofessional, you might consider renting a post office box or adding a suite number to your home address. You might also pay a little extra for a phone number that sounds businesslike (such as 595-1000).

To get you started thinking about your professional image, write your answer to this question in the space below: What do you want your image to say to your potential customers?

_____

_____

_____

_____

Network

There are two ways to network your business: informally and as part of a more structured networking system. Let's consider the informal networking method first.

We are acutely aware of the importance of networking to find a job, or even perhaps a mate, but you should use networking to market your business, too. That means being prepared to talk about your business to anyone and everyone. Your car mechanic may not be interested in buying your product or service, but his brother-in-law might become your best customer. Remember, *business is about relationships.* Always carry your business cards with you, and when you hand them out, give people two: one for themselves and one for someone they know who might be interested in your product or service.

Think of informal networking this way: You probably know at least 100 people and they each probably know at least 100 people. If you contact every person you know and give them two business cards, one for themselves and one for someone they know, you have the possibility of reaching 10,000 people to make them aware of your business.

> **Business is about relationships.**

To get started, simply make a list of people you know and then determine which ones are targeted potential customers. Divide the list with "people you know well" and "people you don't." Start with your friends and family and tell them about your business. By the time you get to the people you don't know as well, your conversations should come easily. Make a few calls a week, introducing them to your business, until you work completely through your list.

This list offers some more ideas to get you started networking informally:

- Become an expert in your field. Newspapers might call for quotes and you'll be asked to speak about your topic.
- Always do what you say you will do. Don't convince people to purchase your product or service until you are ready to deliver the product or service.
- Create a follow-up system so you will remember who and when to call.
- Stay in touch with previous customers.
- Always send thank-you notes.
- Follow up with phone calls after a week to be sure your customers are pleased with your product or service.
- Consider "freebies" if they could lead to sales in the future. If an organization calls for a donation, consider one of your products or your service for the trade-off of a listing in the program.
- Volunteer in local organizations to meet new people in your community.
- Seize each and every opportunity to tell people about your business.

A more structured way of networking is to join a business networking group. You will need to research the various groups that your city offers so you'll know the best ones for you. Here are a few different types of groups to consider:

- **Professional groups:** These groups form to exchange knowledge in a given industry. This type of group is helpful to meet other people in your field. Examples include the National Associates of Manufactures, American Booksellers Association, and National Association of Professional Pet Sitters.
- **Service organizations:** These are usually casual groups that have joined to provide a service in the community. This is a low-key way to get to know people and gradually exchange information. Examples include Kiwanis, Rotary, and Optimists.
- **Social/business organizations:** These groups offer business networking with social activities. Examples include business singles clubs and Jaycees.
- **Business networks:** There are two types of business networks. One is more structured and the main purpose is to pass business referrals among members. They typically allow one member per profession. The other type of business network is less structured and brings many types of businesses together.
- **Online groups:** There are groups on the Internet that may offer you opportunities to network. Some of these include www.linkedin.com, www.ecademy.com, and www.konnects.com

Advertise

Most small businesses don't have the money to pay for an advertising blitz (they simply can't afford a 30-second Super Bowl spot at 2.5 million dollars apiece). The good news is that most small businesses don't *need* to advertise on a large scale. You will probably be better off if you appeal *directly to your target customers* by less-expensive means.

But you still need to include the cost of advertising in your business proposal. As part of your business plan, you need to create a marketing plan with a budget. What methods will you use to let people know about your business and how much will it cost? It's important to create a marketing plan every year, in fact, to stay in control of your advertising and your budget. If you have a plan, it's much easier to resist the salesperson who seems to have a great deal that you really can't afford.

If your business must advertise to larger markets, you should proceed carefully. Many microenterprises have lost vast amounts of money with no return by choosing the wrong advertising vehicles. You might attract more customers with a well-thought-out brochure mailed to people you *know* are potential customers than with a full-page color ad run once in a newspaper.

Here are some basics you should keep in mind, however you choose to advertise:

- Make your message consistent (reinforce your brand).
- Always include the benefit to the customer.
- Create a learning experience for your customers.
- The secret to marketing is repetition.
- Try to create an element of fun.

The following list contains some advertising methods you can consider. Some are more feasible than others for small businesses, but don't discount any of them without exploring all the possibilities.

- **Television** ads are fleeting and hard to do well, and it's difficult to be sure you're going to hit your target market. They also may be too expensive for your small business, but check with local cable stations before you completely rule them out. Cable stations are less expensive and may appeal to an audience that is close to your potential market. Local talk shows also may be perfect for your topic; many interview "experts" on a variety of topics. You may be the expert in your field.

- **Radio** is also expensive, but it's easier to get directly to your target market. Remember, however, that radio usually is background noise, so an ad on the radio takes many repetitions before people actually get your message. Again, talk shows can be helpful in getting your message out.

- **Print advertising** includes ads in either magazines or newspapers. If you do some careful research, you can get directly to your customers with this medium. The impact of print may build more slowly than other kinds of advertising. If your customers will contact you by phone to request your product or service, you might consider an ad in the Yellow Pages. Look at your competitors' ads. But keep this question in mind: How many new customers will you need from that ad each month to make it cost-effective?

- The **press release** is a time-honored way of telling people you're in business, and you don't have to hire a professional to write one. Check your library for information on how a press release should look and what information it should include. Often local media are looking for good stories, so try to present your company as newsworthy. And don't forget to follow up with a phone call to answer questions about your press release. If appropriate, have your services listed in the calendar of events in your local newspaper or in any listing about changes in companies.

- A **Web site** for your business can be an easy and inexpensive way to provide exposure for your business (provided you keep the cost of development under control). Your Internet service provider may offer a Web page free with your subscription. Explore software that provides you with a template to set up your Web page.

Remember, if you have a Web site, you must let your customers know that you're on the Web. Be sure your Web address (URL) is included on all written materials—business cards, stationery, flyers, and so on—and submit it to Internet search engines such as Google (www.google.com) and Yahoo! (www.yahoo.com). For more information on creating a presence on the Web, see the Bonus Chapter on starting an E-business.

- **E-mail** marketing is an inexpensive and effective way to communicate with your customers. Start collecting e-mail addresses from your customers as soon as you start your business. Assure them that you will only use the address to keep them informed about your business and you will not sell your list. You can e-mail your customers information about special sales and new products or send them a monthly newsletter about your business. Be sure and add a link that will allow people to opt out of your e-mails if they choose. Also be sure not to spam—send mass e-mails to people you don't know or who haven't signed up for messages—no matter how tempting it is.

- **Direct mail** is still one of the cheapest ways to get your information into the hands of your customers, but it also is one of the more difficult methods of advertising. If you are going to create a large direct-mail campaign and you don't want your hard work to get thrown out with the junk mail, you need to either thoroughly research your project or hire professional help. If you are mailing to your past customers and your own list of potential customers, always remember to maintain a professional (but eye-catching) image. Again, consult books in the library on setting up a direct-mail campaign.

- **Trade shows** are worth considering if you can find one geared to your products or services. Common estimates say that 86 percent of trade show attendees are there to buy. Your goal should be to meet as many people as possible so you can develop sales leads. Have a system to take names and addresses to add to your customer database, and be sure to follow up on all leads soon after the show.

- **Low cost/no cost marketing.** Word of mouth is probably the best advertising you can have, because your satisfied customers effectively become your sales force. It doesn't cost anything, but it builds slowly. Other low-cost marketing includes donating your product to a fund-raising event; distributing business cards at every opportunity; creating flyers that you can use as bag stuffers or place on bulletin boards; and distributing small giveaways with your logo, such as magnets, bookmarks, or coffee mugs. Get creative about letting your potential customers know that you're ready for business.

What Other Businesses Are Offering the Same Product or Service?

Direct competition is any other business that is selling the same product or service to the same customers that your business is trying to reach.

Once you identify your direct competition, you need to learn everything you can about them. Learn about their products and services, their prices, and what customer service they offer. If you are a retailer, it's easy to visit your competition as a customer. If you're providing a service, call your competition and get a quote. Have a friend or relative actually hire your competitor so they can evaluate the service. If you have no direct competition in your area and there is a similar business in another community, visit them to learn about their operation.

In your research you may discover something your competitors are not doing or that you can do better. Several years ago, two friends opened a balloon delivery service. In calling the competition they quickly realized that competitors were working out of their homes and used answering machines to take messages. Sometimes they didn't call people back until the next day. The two friends knew that people who wanted balloons typically called the same day they wanted the delivery. So they opened a shop with regular hours and answered the phone from 9 am–6 pm. That set them apart from the competition and made their business successful.

To compete, you must find a way to operate the business better, and it's not always a matter of simply having lower prices. Is your competition trying to appeal to the same customers you are? If so, you should try to create a niche. Your niche can be who you serve, what you do, where you do it, when you do it, or how you do it, or it can combine any of those factors, such as a hair salon that specializes in children's haircuts or a dry-cleaners that specializes in pick-up and delivery.

In the following worksheet, list your competitors and identify their strengths and weaknesses. In the space provided, explain how your business is different and will make customers choose you over them. How do you compare with the competition on price, location, quality, service, and image?

My Direct Competitors

Competitor	Strengths	Weaknesses

What makes my business special?

_____

_____

_____

Indirect competition includes businesses that provide an alternative way for customers to meet their needs. These competitors may not be selling exactly the same product or service as yours, but you need to consider them as competition. Ask yourself, if customers do not buy your product or service, where else could they find a product or service that would work just as well? For example, instead of going to your ice-cream parlor, customers might choose low-fat frozen yogurt, fresh-baked cookies, or something they can make at home to satisfy their sweet tooth.

In the space below, jot down any indirect competition you need to consider.

Indirect competition I should consider:

_____

_____

_____

_____

How Will You Deliver Your Product or Service to Keep Customers Coming Back for More?

Americans have become accustomed to horrible shopping experiences. Everyone has stories about a product that was defective, a sales associate who was rude, or feeling lost in a mammoth store with no help in sight. The result is that the bar has been lowered, and customers recognize and appreciate good customer service now more than ever.

As the owner of a small business, you have much more control over the experiences of your customers. You can provide excellent customer service and exceed customers' expectations with every transaction. Whenever you think about dealing with your customers—potential or actual—remember that good customer service can mean the difference between business success and failure. If you have trouble believing that, consider these facts:

- **Customers will tell a company where it needs improvement.** Ask your customers how you can make your business more suitable to them, *and then listen to what they say!* Encourage and welcome suggestions about how you could improve.

- **Poor service is the #1 reason American companies lose business.** Most customers stop doing business with a company because of poor service.

- **Only a minority of dissatisfied customers ever formally complain.** Most dissatisfied customers don't complain because they believe it's not worth their time, the company won't listen, or the company won't do anything about the complaint.

- **Dissatisfied customers tell many people about their dissatisfaction.**

- **It's commonly accepted that it takes $10 of new business to replace $1 of lost business.** It costs more to market to new customers than to maintain old ones. Once you get a customer to try your service or product for the first time, it's important to keep them coming back.

- **Quality of service is the main thing that differentiates one business from another.** Many times the products are so similar that it is how they are delivered that matters.

- **Customers are simply willing to pay more for better service.**

Providing good customer service is actually not all that complicated. The key is to make customers feel important and appreciated. Treat them as individuals, not as transactions. Always use their names and find ways to compliment them, but be sincere. People like doing business with friends! Thank them every chance you get.

Make it easy for your customers to get in touch with you. If you give a potential customer a card, and they call you but you don't return the call for several days, chances are they will have taken their business elsewhere.

If it's possible in your business, throw in something with every purchase. For instance, if you're selling original art work, consider framing it for free. Or if you have a retail business, give all new customers a discount coupon for their return visit. Always try to think like a customer—what would keep *you* coming back? Of course, you need to pay attention to your costs to determine how much you are able to give away.

> **Treat your customers as individuals. Make them feel important and appreciated.**

Finally, take responsibility for your mistakes. When something goes wrong, apologize. It's easy and customers will respect you for it. The customer may not always be right, but it's important that you always allow the customer to win.

Summing Up

You may have the best product or service in your area, but if you have no customers, you will not be able to make money and maintain your business. The time to educate yourself about your product and your potential customers is *before* you begin your business. Ask lots of questions and listen to what people tell you. Remember, you are beginning to make business relationships, so it is important to follow through on your promises.

Marketing is not something you do one time and you're finished. Marketing your business is an ongoing task. Schedule time every day and week to market yourself and your business. Soon you will be bringing in customers and income. The next chapter will teach you how to manage that income.

CHAPTER 7

Managing Your Cash Flow

Successful business owners know how to manage the flow of cash coming into and going out of their businesses. They realize that even a profitable business can fail if no operating cash is available. Skillful cash-flow management results from proper planning. By making some simple forecasts, you can learn to project your cash-flow requirements.

In this chapter, you learn to create useful projections to help you manage your cash flow.

What Is Cash Flow?

Cash flow, as the name implies, is simply the flow of cash coming into and going out of your business. You achieve positive cash flow when money comes into your business faster than it goes out. Because a business must have cash to operate, you must maintain positive cash flow in order to survive. Positive cash flow is a matter of timing. Managing your cash flow is a matter of planning.

Having cash is not the same as being profitable. It is possible for a business to be operating at a loss and still have cash. For example, if you start your business with $10,000 in the bank and you operate at a loss of $1,000 each month, how many months can you stay in business and have cash in the bank? It also is possible for a business to be making a profit and have no cash. For example, if you are operating at a profit and extending 60-day credit terms to your customers but paying your suppliers upon delivery, how long will you be able to keep operating before you run out of cash?

This concept is important to understand, because many small business owners believe that as long as they have cash in the bank, they must be making a profit. That can be a dangerous assumption.

Small business owners tend to neglect the task of business management. There are many important things a business owner must do: make sales, produce products, provide services, compete for customers. Owners often spend so much time "being" the business that they don't take time to "manage" the business. This is a common mistake that results in the business "managing" the owner.

Manage your business, or your business will manage you.

As a business owner, you will probably face cash-flow management tasks daily. If you don't start with a plan, you'll spend a great deal of time reacting to instead of anticipating events. You may find yourself trying to placate suppliers, struggling to make loan payments, hoping for a miracle so you can make payroll, and losing sleep over how to keep your utilities from being disconnected (again). The result is that you have even less time to make sales, produce products, provide services, and compete for customers—plus you will have strained important relationships with your creditors.

In the long run, you create more stress for yourself if you don't manage your business. Avoid the trap of being managed by your business: Learn to manage your cash flow.

Projecting Cash Flow

Take a look at an example of a mismanaged business. Like so many business owners, Cathy Smith, the owner of Cathy's Cleaning Service, believes she has no time to project and manage her cash flow.

Cathy's Cleaning Service

Cathy Smith owns a residential and commercial cleaning business. She has four part-time employees (one of whom is her mother) who work in two cleaning crews. Each crew works the same monthly schedule, cleaning two commercial buildings and seven homes.

Cathy also cleans newly constructed homes for a local builder and vacated apartments for a property management company. She cleans these herself.

Her residential customers pay for cleaning services as they are performed by leaving checks for the crews to deliver to Cathy at the end of each day. The two commercial buildings are invoiced once a month with 30-day terms. Cathy invoices the construction company and property manager as she cleans for them, and they usually pay her within 15 days.

Cathy reimburses her employees for mileage expenses to travel to job sites. She includes these reimbursements with the paychecks each Friday afternoon.

Cathy has no cash-flow plan; she is much too busy cleaning to create one each month.

Let's look at Cathy's cash flow for the month of August.

Cathy's Cleaning Service, Before...

Week 1	Ending Bank Balance
Cathy starts the week with $75.	$75.00
1. She collects $180 from residential homes.	$255.00
2. Cathy gets a check for $280 for new homes cleaned two weeks ago.	$535.00
3. Payroll this week is $435.	$100.00
4. Mileage reimbursements total is $40.	$60.00
5. Cathy needs $25 to reimburse herself for mileage.	$35.00
Cathy ends week one with $35.	$35.00

Week 2

6. Residential homes pay $225 this week.	$260.00
7. A new home Cathy cleaned two weeks ago pays $70.	$330.00
8. Payroll is $435, which leaves Cathy short. She asks her mother not to cash her check, but her mother cannot afford to do this.	($105.00)
9. Employee mileage reimbursements are $40. Cathy isn't sure what to do.	($145.00)
Cathy ends the week with a negative bank balance and worries that the checks will hit the bank before she can cover them.	($145.00)

Week 3

10. Cathy hears from the bank immediately: Her account is charged a $35 NSF fee.	($180.00)
11. Cathy borrows $200 from a friend, who is not happy about it.	$20.00
12. Residential homes pay $180.	$200.00
13. Building No. 2 pays $400 for one month.	$600.00
14. Payroll this week is $435. Employees murmur and rush to the bank.	$165.00
15. Employee mileage reimbursements are $40.	$125.00
16. Cathy must spend $50 on cleaning supplies.	$75.00
17. Cathy needs $12.50 for gas for her car (she can't afford to fill 'er up).	$62.50
18. An apartment she cleaned last month pays her $82.	$144.50
Cathy ends this week with $144.50, an angry friend, upset employees, and a serious headache.	$144.50

Week 4

19. Cathy collects $225 from residential customers.	$369.50
20. Building No. 1 pays a $440 monthly cleaning bill.	$809.50
21. Payroll is $435, and Cathy is thrilled she has the cash.	$374.50
22. Cathy's angry friend insists on repayment of the $200 loan now!	$174.50
23. Employee mileage reimbursements total $40.	$134.50
24. A new home Cathy cleaned two weeks ago pays $100.	$234.50
25. Cathy needs gas for her car again: $25.	$209.50
26. Cathy finally pays herself a salary for the month: $150.	$59.50
Cathy ends the month with $59.50 and the dread of facing another month of similar struggles!	

Cathy Makes a Plan

1. Cathy knows how much and when she will collect from residential customers.

2. Cathy's payroll amount remains about the same each week.

3. Her commercial accounts are on contract and pay the same amount each month.

4. Cathy knows about how much she will have to reimburse her employees for mileage.

5. Cathy can make an educated guess about how much income she will collect from cleaning new houses and vacant apartments. She also can ask the new homes builder and the apartment manager to give her an estimate at the beginning of each month, because they know when they will need her weeks before they call her.

Given all that Cathy knows and can assume, she can draw a "picture" of when cash is going to come in and when it is going to go out. It would look like the table below.

Cathy's Cleaning Service

Date	Description	Cash In	Cash Out	Balance
				$75.00
Week 1	Homes	$180.00		$255.00
		$180.00		$255.00
	New Homes	$280.00		$535.00
	Payroll		$435.00	$100.00
	Mileage		$40.00	$60.00
	Gasoline		$25.00	$35.00
Week 2	Homes	$225.00		$260.00
	New Home	$70.00		$330.00
	Payroll		$435.00	($105.00)
	Mileage		$40.00	($145.00)
Week 3	NSF		$35.00	($180.00)
	Loan	$200.00		$20.00
	Homes	$180.00		$200.00
	Building #2	$400.00		$600.00
	Payroll		$435.00	$165.00
	Mileage		$40.00	$125.00
	Cleaning Sup		$50.00	$75.00
	Gasoline		$12.50	$62.50
	Apartment	$82.00		$144.50
Week 4	Homes	$225.00		$369.50
	Building #1	$440.00		$809.50
	Payroll		$435.00	$374.50
	Repay Loan		$200.00	$174.50
	Mileage		$40.00	$134.50
	New Home	$100.00		$234.50
	Gasoline		$25.00	$209.50
	Cathy's Salary		$150.00	$59.50
		$2,382.00	**$2,397.50**	**$59.50**

Without any plan, Cathy didn't *know* she was going to run out of cash. After she creates her plan, she is better able to come up with some short-term solutions for her anticipated cash shortages. More importantly, Cathy has seen the need to come up with some long-term solutions to avoid future cash shortages.

Here are some other ideas that might help Cathy improve her cash-flow plan:

1. Cathy invoices her commercial customers only once a month, even though she cleans for them every week. They pay her invoices according to her terms: within 30 days. Cathy could start sending invoices on a weekly basis. The invoice amounts would be smaller (one week of cleaning instead of one month), but the payments would come in faster.

> **Rules for positive cash flow:**
> **1. Schedule cash to come in sooner.**
> **2. Hang on to cash longer.**

2. Cathy pays her employees and reimburses their mileage expenses once a week. She could change her payroll and mileage reimbursements to once every two weeks (26 times per year) or, better yet, twice a month (24 times per year). This would allow Cathy to hold on to her cash longer.

3. Instead of paying for her supplies in cash, Cathy could establish credit accounts with her primary suppliers. Again, Cathy would hold on to her cash longer.

In the tables on the following pages, you can see the effects of these three simple changes on Cathy's cash flow.

Notice that Cathy didn't collect any more cash from her commercial accounts, she just collected it *faster*. She did not pay her employees any less, she just *held on to her cash longer*. Cathy still was able to buy cleaning supplies when she needed them, she just *deferred payment*.

As a result of these changes, Cathy didn't bounce any payroll checks, which made her employees happy. She didn't need to borrow money from her friend, which made her friend happy. She avoided the bank's NSF charges, which made her bank happy. And she was left with considerably higher cash balances at the end of each week, which made *her* happy. She also begins the new month with a higher cash balance and a management plan.

Cathy's Cleaning Service, Before...

Date	Description	Cash In	Cash Out	Balance
				$75.00
Week 1	Homes	$180.00		$255.00
	New Homes	$280.00		$535.00
	Payroll		$435.00	$100.00
	Mileage		$40.00	$60.00
	Gasoline		$25.00	$35.00
Week 2	Homes	$225.00		$260.00
	New Home	$70.00		$330.00
	Payroll		$435.00	($105.00)
	Mileage		$40.00	($145.00)
Week 3	NSF		$35.00	($180.00)
	Loan	$200.00		$20.00
	Homes	$180.00		$200.00
	Building #2	$400.00		$600.00
	Payroll		$435.00	$165.00
	Mileage		$40.00	$125.00
	Cleaning Sup		$50.00	$75.00
	Gasoline		$12.50	$62.50
	Apartment	$82.00		$144.50
Week 4	Homes	$225.00		$369.50
	Building #1	$440.00		$809.50
	Payroll		$435.00	$374.50
	Repay Loan		$200.00	$174.50
	Mileage		$40.00	$134.50
	New Home	$100.00		$234.50
	Gasoline		$25.00	$209.50
	Cathy's Salary		$150.00	$59.50
		$2,382.00	**$2,397.50**	**$59.50**

Cathy's Cleaning Service, After

Date	Description	Cash In	Cash Out	Balance
				$75.00
Week 1	Homes	$180.00		$255.00
	New Homes	$280.00		$535.00
	Building #1	$100.00		$635.00
	Building #2	$110.00		$745.00
	Gasoline		$25.00	$720.00
Week 2	Homes	$225.00		$945.00
	New Home	$70.00		$1,015.00
	Building #1	$100.00		$1,115.00
	Building #2	$110.00		$1,225.00
	Payroll/2 wks		$870.00	$355.00
	Mileage/2 wks		$80.00	$275.00
Week 3	Homes	$180.00		$455.00
	Building #1	$100.00		$555.00
	Building #2	$110.00		$665.00
	Apartment	$82.00		$747.00
	Gasoline		$12.50	$734.50
Week 4	Homes	$225.00		$959.50
	Building #1	$100.00		$1,059.50
	Building #2	$110.00		$1,169.50
	Payroll/2 wks		$870.00	$299.50
	Mileage/2 wks		$80.00	$219.50
	New Home	$100.00		$319.50
	Gasoline		$25.00	$294.50
	Cathy's Salary		$150.00	$144.50
		$2,182.00	**$2,112.50**	**$144.50**

Cathy saved herself the $35.00 NSF fee, plus she owes a supplier $50.00 for cleaning supplies, which is payable in 30 days.

Improving Cash Flow

There are two simple rules for managing the cash flow in your small business:

1. Schedule your cash to come in sooner.

2. Hang on to your cash longer.

Below are some specific strategies that will help you follow these rules:

- **Bill frequently.** This follows the rule for scheduling cash to come in faster. Bill smaller amounts more frequently rather than waiting for the full amount to come in at a later date.

- **Check your customer's credit references.** Before extending credit to customers, ask them to complete a credit application, complete with references. Be sure to check their references to determine whether they pay their accounts on time. Don't extend credit to customers with a history of slow pays.

- **Stay on top of collections.** The moment a customer payment is late, pick up the phone and call. Tell them that you are just following up on the status of their payment. If they tell you they've already mailed the payment, ask for the date and check number. Follow up often in a firm but friendly manner. If the check doesn't arrive within a few days, call again. This is one case where the squeaky wheel really does get the grease! Small businesses cannot afford to let credit extended to customers go beyond the due date!

- **Collect deposits.** When possible, ask customers to place deposits on purchases, particularly if you have to special order items. Be sure to track deposits carefully so you know the status of each customer account.

- **Sell gift cards and gift certificates.** Collecting money up front for a product or service that doesn't have to be delivered until much later can be an effective cash flow management strategy. Just be certain to track the amount of certificates you've sold so you have the required inventory on hand or time to deliver services when the certificates are redeemed. Be sure to print expiration dates on the gift certificates!

- **Sell service agreements.** Service agreements are a good way to generate extra income and cash flow at the time of a sale. If you sell a reliable product line, you may never have to service many of the items you sell. Even service providers can sell service agreements. For example, an HVAC service company may sell a contract in March to service a customer's air conditioner at the beginning of the cooling season and their furnace at the beginning of the heating season. They collect the money early in the year and sell two services at the same time!

- **Sell memberships.** Membership fees are an excellent way to generate positive cash flow.

- **Bundle products.** Bundle fast-selling items (for example, a computer system) with other items that complement it (software, a printer, paper, a flash drive, a surge protector, and cables). Not only do you improve your cash flow but you substantially increase your sales income. Bundling also helps you move inventory that might not otherwise sell.

- **Offer low price specials; sell upgrades.** Car dealerships and electronics stores are masters of this strategy. They get the customer in the door with an advertisement of a low-priced item—for example, the $119/mo. car with no air conditioning and no floor mats. They soon entice the customer to buy the upgraded version, complete with bells and whistles. This increases sales volume and improves cash flow at the same time.

- **Offer customers small incentives for early payment.** Offer customers small discounts if they pay early; for example, 2%/10 Net 30 is a common credit term that means if the customer pays the bill in 10 days, they can take a 2% discount. If they pay in 30 days, they must pay the full amount (net). Another strategy is to offer to waive the shipping fee (if you ship items to customers) for prepaid orders.

- **Don't pay your bills early.** When cash is tight, do not take advantage of incentives to pay your bills early; hang on to your cash longer by waiting the full credit term and paying the full amount of the bill on time.

- **Consider leasing instead of buying equipment.** Making monthly lease payments allows you to hang on to your cash longer than paying a lump sum for a large purchase.

- **Carry a smaller inventory.** Excess inventory gathering dust is a poor use of your money. Most suppliers are very responsive and can deliver products within a short lead time. Don't spend cash you should be hanging on to for inventory that you can't move quickly.

Predicting the (Cash) Future

It doesn't take a crystal ball to project your cash future. What it does take is some educated guessing. The longer you are in business and the more experience you acquire, the better your guesses will be.

To create cash-flow projections, take the information you know plus information you can assume and apply it to a calendar or a time line. Not all businesses are as predictable as Cathy's Cleaning Service. Some information may be easy to predict: For example, your rent is a fixed amount that is due on the first day of each month; your telephone bill rarely fluctuates and is always due on the 25th; and your insurance premiums are payable once a quarter. Other information is more difficult to forecast: How much will sales revenues be in January? Will this be a harsh winter with extraordinarily high heating bills? Will you suffer costly equipment failures?

When preparing your cash-flow projections, there are other things to consider, as well. Will seasonal fluctuations, holidays, or events in your community have an impact on your business? Will a convention in town mean more or less business for you? What about sporting events? How about plans for road construction? Will the weather affect your business? What about annual conventions for your industry?

Whether you are establishing a new business or managing an existing one, think of ways to stretch your dollars to improve your cash flow. This might mean renegotiating credit terms with customers or suppliers. If this is the case, schedule time to do it. Remember, time spent managing your business ensures that your business does not manage you!

Tip: There are computer programs available that can make preparing cash-flow projections easier, including electronic spreadsheets (such as Microsoft Excel) and simple-to-use accounting software (such as the Quicken and QuickBooks products by Intuit, Inc.). Whether you do projections manually or on a computer, you need to gather and calculate the same information.

Sandra's Sewing Circle

In this exercise, account for start-up cash flow in and start-up cash flow out; then estimate four consecutive weeks of operation in a new business. Complete the Start-Up Business Cash-Flow Worksheet using these assumptions:

1. Sandra's Sewing Circle begins with a cash balance of $0.00. She will make an owner's investment of $1,000 and add a no-interest loan from her mother of $500.

2. Sandra will have to pay an $80 deposit to the phone company for service, as well as a $50 business license fee to the city.

3. Sandra will purchase $450 of start-up inventory. She already owns most of her own equipment, and she is setting up her business in a friend's shop.

4. Sandra is now ready to start estimating her operating expenses. In the first week, Sandra will begin paying her friend $40 a week for rent. Sandra thinks she will do $120 of business, for which she will be paid in cash. Sandra will have to pay $75 for a previous delivery of business cards and stationery. She estimates an additional purchase of fabrics for $40.

5. In her second week of business, Sandra estimates income of $145. She estimates that her share of the electric bill will be $20. She knows she will have an insurance premium of $75. Sandra wants to draw $150 for her own salary. Additional fabrics should be around $50.

6. In week 3, Sandra hopes to bring in $200 of sales income from a high school band account, as well as $45 of retail business. She will pay for an ad in the neighborhood newspaper, which will cost $25. She estimates a purchase of fabrics at a cost of $75.

7. Sandra estimates income of only $120 in week 4. Sandra will have to pay her mother $200 against her loan this week. She also wants to pay herself another $150. Sandra estimates her telephone bill at $60 and additional fabrics at $40.

On the following pages are two start-up cash-flow worksheets and one cash-flow worksheet for an existing business. Complete the first start-up worksheet using the information about Sandra's Sewing Circle. Use the other worksheets to make cash-flow projections for your own business.

Start-Up Business Cash-Flow Worksheet

	Start-up cash flow	Week 1	Week 2	Week 3	Week 4
1. Beginning cash					
Cash in					
2. Owner's investment					
3. Loan proceeds					
4. Sales income					
5. Other:					
6. Total cash in (add lines 2–5)					
Cash out/start-up					
7. Initial rent/deposits					
8. Initial utility/deposits					
9. Equipment purchases/deposits					
10. Initial inventory purchases					
11. Initial office supply purchases					
12. Fees/License					
13. Other:					
Cash out					
14. COGS, labor					
15. COGS, materials					
16. Rent					
17. Insurance					
18. Payroll					
19. Payroll taxes					
20. Loan payments					
21. Advertising/Marketing					
22. Travel expenses					
23. Owner's compensation					
24. Office supplies					
25. Telephone					
26. Utilities					
27. Other:					
28. Other:					
29. Total cash out (add lines 7–28)					
30. Change in cash (line 6 minus line 29)					
31. Ending cash (line 1 plus line 30)					

Note: Ending cash for one period becomes the beginning cash for the next period.

Start-Up Business Cash-Flow Worksheet

	Start-up cash flow	Week 1	Week 2	Week 3	Week 4
1. Beginning cash					
Cash in					
2. Owner's investment					
3. Loan proceeds					
4. Sales income					
5. Other:					
6. Total cash in (add lines 2–5)					
Cash out/start-up					
7. Initial rent/deposits					
8. Initial utility/deposits					
9. Equipment purchases/deposits					
10. Initial inventory purchases					
11. Initial office supply purchases					
12. Fees/License					
13. Other:					
Cash out					
14. COGS, labor					
15. COGS, materials					
16. Rent					
17. Insurance					
18. Payroll					
19. Payroll taxes					
20. Loan payments					
21. Advertising/Marketing					
22. Travel expenses					
23. Owner's compensation					
24. Office supplies					
25. Telephone					
26. Utilities					
27. Other:					
28. Other:					
29. Total cash out (add lines 7–28)					
30. Change in cash (line 6 minus line 29)					
31. Ending cash (line 1 plus line 30)					

Note: Ending cash for one period becomes the beginning cash for the next period.

Existing Business Cash-Flow Worksheet

	Period 1		Period 2		Period 3	
	Projected	Actual	Projected	Actual	Projected	Actual
1. Beginning cash						
Cash in						
2. Owner's investment						
3. Loan proceeds						
4. Sales income						
5. Other:						
6. Total cash in (add lines 2–5)						
Cash out						
7. COGS, labor						
8. COGS, materials						
9. Rent						
10. Insurance						
11. Payroll						
12. Payroll taxes						
13. Loan payments						
14. Advertising/Marketing						
15. Travel expenses						
16. Owner's compensation						
17. Office supplies						
18. Telephone						
19. Utilities						
20. Other:						
21. Other:						
22. Other:						
23. Other:						
24. Other:						
25. Total cash out (add lines 7–24)						
26. Change in cash (line 6 minus line 25)						
27. Ending cash (line 1 plus line 26)						

Note: Ending cash for one period becomes the beginning cash for the next period.

Projections for Lenders

If you intend to approach a lender for funds, a *cash-flow projection* will be an important part of your financial plan. You should make your cash-flow projection for at least one year, maybe longer, depending on the requirements of the lender.

It is common for a start-up business to show negative cash balances in the first year. Most lenders expect your projections to show a cash break-even point within the first year and show positive cash flow in subsequent years. You must be prepared to show the lender how you plan to handle negative cash flow. Are you seeking a loan or a line of credit to cover the entire negative cash balance? Do you also have personal resources you will be contributing? Do you have investors with available cash?

Because projections are only estimates of what will happen, it's a good idea to submit at least three projections for the same period: a worst-case scenario, a likely scenario, and a best-case scenario. Be as realistic as possible in your projections. (Many lenders will still discount your projections as too optimistic.)

If you are seeking a loan, your projections must include a "cash in" line to show the loan proceeds coming into the business. Identify how those proceeds will be spent under "cash out." Will there be equipment or inventory purchases? Don't forget to include another "cash out" line reflecting your scheduled loan payments. Your lender will look for indications that you will use the loan proceeds to generate income. He or she also will evaluate how wisely you are using cash. Obviously, your projections must demonstrate an ability to pay back the loan. Ask your accountant or business advisor to review your projections before you submit them.

Summing Up

Cash-flow management can be a challenge in a small business. The key to effective cash-flow management is proper planning, which allows you to anticipate events—not just react to them. Remember: Manage your business, or your business will manage you!

In the next chapter you will decide what form your business should take and the implications of that decision.

CHAPTER 8

The Business of Business

How do you make your business legal? Should you incorporate? Or should you operate your business as a sole proprietor? In this chapter, we consider the legal forms of businesses so you can determine which suits you best. It's important to choose one that will save you taxes and provide you with adequate liability protection. You will also need to research your state's requirements to determine the details of creating and maintaining your business.

In this chapter, we also look at the special insurance needs of a new business, examine different types of insurance, discuss how to create a plan that meets your needs, and consider some important criteria for choosing an insurance agent.

Legal Forms of Business

You can choose from several types of business entities. The most popular for small businesses are sole proprietorships, general partnerships, limited liability companies, and corporations. Let's examine each of these in more detail.

Sole Proprietorships

The simplest form of business is a *sole proprietorship,* which merely indicates that the business is owned and run by an individual acting alone. The owner has total control, keeps all the profits, and is responsible for all the taxes and liabilities of the business. If the owner dies or is incapacitated, the business ceases to function. The owner is personally responsible for debts and obligations of the business. Here is a list of some of the advantages and disadvantages of this kind of business.

Advantages
- It requires the least amount of red tape to create and run.
- It is the least expensive to set up.
- You are your own boss.

Disadvantages
- You are completely responsible for all aspects of the business.
- Getting outside investments is difficult.
- Any debts or claims brought against the business are your personal responsibility.

Tax Issues

- A sole proprietorship does not pay taxes and does not have to file a tax return with the IRS. Instead, all profits or losses of the business are "passed through" the business to the business owner, who reports them on a Schedule C attached to his or her personal income tax return (Form 1040).

- All profits generated by the business are taxable income to the business owner, regardless of whether the owner takes them in the form of compensation or leaves them in the business.

- Any money the business owner takes out of the business in the form of compensation (or salary) is considered profit and taxable as income.

- All profits are subject to payment of Self Employment Tax. This represents both the employee's and the employer's share of social security and Medicare taxes. The self-employment tax rate for 2007 is 15.3% of the first $97,500 of income and 2.9% of everything over $97,500.

  For more information, see the Internal Revenue Publication 334, Tax Guide for Small Business.

Forming a Sole Proprietorship

- It's very simple to form a sole proprietorship. There are no state or federal forms to file. You may do business using your own name, or you may operate your business using a "fictitious" name, such as Maggie May's Mending.

- If you choose a fictitious name, check with your Secretary of State to see if the name is available and what you may have to do to register this name on behalf of your business.

- You will have to secure any business licenses or permits that your state, city, or county may require. Check with your Secretary of State or local SBA office for more information.

- You do not have to apply for an Employer Identification Number (EIN) with the Internal Revenue Service unless you have employees. Still, it's not a bad idea to get an EIN so that you can use this number when you open your business checking account (see chapter 9 for more information about EINs).

- If your business collects sales tax, pays employees, or pays excise tax, you will have to apply for a state tax ID number with your state Department of Revenue. Check with your local Secretary of State or SBA office for more information about what your state requires.

- Most Secretary of State Offices offer small business information packets that outline the requirements for forming a sole proprietorship.

General Partnerships

A *general partnership* is two or more people working as co-owners of a business for profit. Think of two sole-proprietors co-owning a business: Both partners are responsible for all the liabilities and debts of the business. The dissolution of a partnership may be caused by the death, bankruptcy, or withdrawal of a partner.

Advantages

- Partners share the profits of the business, motivating both to apply their best efforts.
- Partners have each other to share the responsibilities, challenges, and successes of the business.

Disadvantages

- The partners share unlimited liability for the business.
- Each partner is responsible for his or her own actions, as well as the actions of other partners and employees of the business.
- It's difficult to obtain large sums of capital.

Tax Issues

- Partnerships, like sole proprietorships, are "pass-through" entities: profits or losses are passed through to the partners and declared on their personal income tax returns.
- Profits or losses are passed through to the individual partners in proportion to each partner's ownership share.
- The partnership itself does not pay taxes, but it is required to file an information tax return (Form 1065).
- Profits are subject to self-employment taxes.

Forming a General Partnership

- Forming a general partnership is a simple process, very similar to forming a sole proprietorship. Check with your Secretary of State's office for instructions.
- General partnerships should operate under a written agreement that specifies details such as how profits and losses will be distributed among the partners, how the business will be managed, and how existing partners can withdraw from or new partners be added to the business. Sample general partnership agreements can be found online, but it's a good idea to have an attorney review your partnership agreement.

Limited Liability Company (LLC)

A *limited liability company,* commonly called an LLC, is a business structure that combines the best features of a sole proprietorship or partnership with those of a corporation: It offers pass-through taxation like a partnership, and limited personal liability for the debts and actions of the business like a corporation.

Owners of an LLC are called *members*. In most states, members may include individuals, corporations, and other LLCs. There is no maximum number of members. Most states permit single-member LLCs but a few states require at least two members.

Advantages

- Pass-through taxation: Profits or losses are divided among the owners and are declared on their personal income tax returns.
- LLC members are protected from personal liability for business debts and claims. If the LLC can't pay a creditor, such as a supplier or a landlord, the creditor cannot

legally come after the LLC members' houses, cars, or other personal assets. Because only LLC assets are used to pay off business debts, LLC members stand to lose only the money that they've invested in the LLC. This is referred to as *limited liability.*

- It is relatively easy to convert a sole proprietorship or partnership to an LLC. Some states provide a form called a *certificate of conversion.*

Disadvantages

- Not all businesses can operate as an LLC. A business in the banking, trust, and insurance industries is typically prohibited from forming an LLC. Some states, including California, prohibit professionals such as architects, accountants, doctors, and other licensed health-care workers from forming an LLC.
- If a written operating agreement is not part of the articles of organization, the LLC will be governed by the default rules in the filing state.

Tax Issues

- The LLC does not pay any income taxes itself. Instead, each LLC owner pays taxes on their share of profits or deducts their share of losses on their personal tax returns.
- A single-member LLC is taxed as a sole proprietorship. The business is not required to file a tax return. The business owner reports business profits on a Schedule C attached to his or her 1040 tax return.
- An LLC with more than one member is automatically classified as a partnership by default and should file the partnership tax return (1065). Profits are passed through to the members and reported on a Schedule C attached to their 1040 personal tax returns.
- Multi-owner LLCs may elect to have the LLC taxed as a C corporation. Check with your accountant to see whether this election makes sense for your business. You will need to file Form 8832 with the IRS. Once your C corporation tax status is approved, your accountant will file the C corporation tax return for your LLC.
- Multi-owner LLCs may elect to have the LLC taxed as an S corporation. Again, your accountant should advise you in this matter. To elect S corporation tax status for your LLC, file Form 2553 with the IRS. Once your S corporation tax status is approved, your accountant will file an S corporation tax return for your business.

Forming a Limited Liability Corporation

- LLCs file Articles (or Certificates) of Organization through their Secretary of State's office. Some states require that you publish your intent to form an LLC. Multi-owner LLCs should create an Operating Agreement that outlines the rights and responsibilities of the owners. (You may want to consult an attorney to draft, or at least review, your operating agreement.) The Operating Agreement should be filed along with the Articles of Organization.
- The name of the LLC should comply with the rules outlined by your Secretary of State's office.

Corporations

Corporations are separate legal entities that exist apart from the people who own or run the corporation. A corporation gives its owners limited liability: If the corporation is sued and a judgment is entered against it, the owners' personal assets (cars, homes, etc.) cannot be used to pay the corporation's debt. The business owners stand to lose only the amount of money they've invested in the corporation.

Because corporations are considered legal entities having their own rights and responsibilities, they can sue and be sued, own assets, borrow money, file bankruptcy, and transfer ownership.

A corporation is managed by a board of directors, which is elected by shareholders. The board of directors, in turn, elects officers to run the day-to-day operations of the business. An important characteristic of a corporation is continuity of life; that is, it may continue to exist indefinitely (as long as certain requirements are met) and not be affected by the death of officers, directors, or shareholders. Interests in corporations are freely transferable (owners can sell their stock), and shareholders are not personally liable for the debts and obligations of the corporation, unless the articles of incorporation provide otherwise.

In order to maintain the limited liability of shareholders, a corporation must observe the corporate formalities of keeping records; holding meetings of the shareholders and the board of directors; paying appropriate taxes; and filing required documents with the Secretary of State, including annual reports. The failure to properly organize a corporation can subject the shareholders to personal liability. If a corporation fails to operate as a corporation, its creditors may attempt to "pierce the corporate veil" (see chapter 9) and make claims against the shareholders personally.

Below are the advantages, disadvantages, and tax ramifications of a corporation followed by more detail on the different types of corporations: S corporations, C corporations, and nonprofit corporations.

Advantages

- In general, corporations have a much easier time getting investors.
- Corporations have a legal existence separate from the owners or investors.
- If one or more of the officers, directors, or shareholders leaves or dies, the business continues to exist.
- The corporation, not the individuals involved, is liable for any losses. Each person can lose only what he or she has invested.
- Liability is limited (but see the Disadvantages section).

Disadvantages

- New corporations often cannot get credit without the owners making personal guarantees.
- There is more red tape to form a corporation. Most people use an attorney to draft their Articles of Incorporation, which adds cost.
- There are rules that must be followed to maintain corporate status.

Tax Issues

- With a C corporation, taxable income is taxed at a corporate tax rate and paid by the corporation, which files its own tax return. After these taxes are paid, distributions made to stockholders are taxed again at the stockholder's tax rate for dividends. This is referred to as *double taxation*. Since corporations have their own tax rate structure, in some cases, C corporations make financial sense despite double taxation. Consult with an accounting professional to determine whether a C corporation makes sense for your business.

- For a Subchapter S corporation, the profits or losses are divided among the shareholders, who then report their portion of the profits or losses (whether they take them out of the corporation or leave them in the company) on their personal income taxes.

Other Issues Related to S Corporations

- A corporation can elect to be an S corporation if it is a domestic corporation with no more than 100 shareholders (husbands and wives count as 1) and its owners are individuals, estates, exempt organizations, and certain trusts. The corporation can have no nonresident alien shareholders and has only one class of stock. Most banks, insurance companies, professional corporations, and certain other corporations may not qualify for S corporation status. Check with your accountant to see whether your business qualifies.

- An S corporation also may not be a member of an affiliated group, which means that an S corporation may not own another corporation.

Nonprofit Corporations

While a for-profit business exists to earn a profit for its owners and shareholders, a nonprofit organization exists to serve a social cause. Nonprofits must apply for federal nonprofit status, at which time they are required to specify—in great detail—how their organization's mission benefits society. These applications undergo close scrutiny; only organizations with a legitimate nonprofit purpose are likely to be approved. Following are some key points regarding nonprofit corporations:

- All money the nonprofit earns can only be used to further its mission. Any profit it earns must go back into the organization. Individuals cannot claim an ownership stake in a nonprofit organization; therefore, profits cannot be distributed to any owners.

- Nonprofit corporations may apply for both federal and state tax-exempt status. The formation documents must include certain information, such as a very detailed business purpose statement. It is recommended you consult an attorney experienced at submitting nonprofit applications if you are interested in forming such a corporation.

- A nonprofit must create a board of directors responsible for the management of the organization. The board sets the salary and benefits for the staff. Directors are typically not personally responsible for the debts and liabilities of the nonprofit corporation.

- Certain nonprofit corporations are eligible to receive public and private grants, making capital easier to attain. However, there is a tremendous amount of paperwork related to maintaining corporate status and obtaining funds.

- With 501(c)(3) nonprofits, donations made by individuals to the nonprofit corporation are tax-deductible.

- The nonprofit is not "owned" by its founders, so it cannot be sold. If the nonprofit dissolves, its assets must be given to another nonprofit organization.

A business owner cannot start a small business and try to designate it as "nonprofit" thinking this will allow him or her to avoid paying taxes, tap into "free" grant money as a source of income, or somehow continue to stay in business despite never realizing a profit.

Forming a Corporation

The following steps are necessary to form a corporation:

1. Choose a name that is available (check availability through your Secretary of State's office) and complies with your state rules for a corporation name. Most states require the name to include one of the following: "Corporation," "Corp.," "Incorporated," "Inc.," "Limited," or "Ltd."

2. Appoint a board of directors. Check with your state to see how many directors you must have. Some states allow corporations with only one owner to have only one director. Owners may usually appoint themselves as directors.

3. File paperwork with your state and pay the filing fee. Most states require you to complete Articles of Incorporation. These don't have to be complicated and can often consist of filling in a form your Secretary of State can provide. The business owner or owners may sign the Articles of Incorporation as the *incorporator*. Most states require you to name a *registered agent*. This is the person to whom all legal and tax paperwork will be mailed and is the stated contact person in public records. The registered agent can be the business owner or an attorney.

4. Create your corporate bylaws. These are the rules by which your corporation will operate. It is often a good idea to have an attorney draft (or at least review) your corporate bylaws.

5. Obtain any local or state licenses or permits your business requires.

6. Hold your initial board of directors meeting. At this meeting, the board will adopt the bylaws, appoint officers, and authorize shares of stock to be issued.

7. Issue stock certificates to the initial shareholders of your corporation (this may be just one person: you, the business owner).

Corporations are legal entities that are required to observe certain formalities in order to retain their status (and their limited liability protection). A small business attorney can advise you on establishing and maintaining your corporation.

For more information about choosing, establishing, and maintaining different legal forms of business, visit the business structures section of www.nolo.com.

Choose the Best Business Form

Read through the following scenarios and decide which would be the best business form for each: sole proprietorship, partnership, limited liability company, S corporation, C corporation, or nonprofit corporation.

Susan's Secretarial Service

Susan has been a legal secretary working for the same attorney for the last 10 years. He is retiring at the end of the year, so Susan must make a career move. For years she has dreamed of owning her own business, and she thinks this might be a good time to pursue that dream. She knows several people in the legal community, and she knows that most law firms have an overabundance of work. She thinks she can contract with several firms for some of their overload. She wants to work from her home and already has all of the necessary equipment to get started.

What would be the best legal business form for her? _____

Movin' on Down the Road

Nicholas graduated from college six months ago and has been looking for a job ever since. He has been forced to move back home, and his parents are beginning to lose patience with him. His friend Michael spent the last five summers working for a large moving company and now has big plans to open his own moving company. His idea is to concentrate on local moves for individuals and office moves for companies. Michael has done his homework, is sure of his market, and has convinced Nicholas to go into the business with him on a 50-50 basis.

What would be the best legal business form for them? _____

Hogin, Johnson, & Associates

Darlene Hogin and Cynthia Johnson are good friends who work for a community development corporation (CDC). Darlene's main responsibility is writing proposals to government agencies and private foundations requesting funding for CDC programs and operations. Cynthia is the vice-president of operations. Darlene and Cynthia are unhappy working for their organization and decide to strike out on their own as consultants to other CDCs. With their combined skills, they're sure they will be successful.

What would be the best legal business form for them? _____

Pamper Your Pet

Kathy and Mark Smith are devoted pet lovers. They both have high-paying jobs, but neither is very happy with his or her career path. They've talked about starting a family, but they can't imagine how they will care for a child because they both work such long hours.

Last Sunday, Kathy saw an ad in the paper for a pet grooming business that is for sale. She called the following morning. The owner said he would be willing to stay on until Kathy is completely trained. The price sounds fair. If Mark keeps his job and Kathy starts the new business, they can make it financially and maybe start that family. They agree to move ahead with the idea.

What would be the best legal business form for them? _____

Designs by Debbie

Debbie has always considered herself an artist. She has a good computer with several graphic design programs, and she continually upgrades her equipment and software. She loves designing and creating all kinds of paper products. Several friends have asked her to make invitations to parties. She has even produced wedding invitations. Sometimes her friends offer to pay her, but she doesn't feel right taking money for something she loves doing.

Recently, her friends have encouraged her to test the market to see if there is a niche for her design business. She is reluctant, but she is tempted by the idea of making money in her own business doing the work she loves so much.

What would be the best legal business form for her? _____

Ben's Best Brew

Ben has a beer recipe he is convinced would be a best seller. He has tested it out on many friends, and all agree that it has a great and unusual taste. Ben has done a lot of research, and he's found that it would take about $200,000 to start producing and marketing his product. He has a well-written and well-thought-out business plan, and he has approached several banks, but he hasn't been able to generate any interest.

So Ben decides to approach some of his friends to see if they might be interested in buying stock in his company. He invites several friends to a Sunday brunch at his house (serving his own beer, of course) to explain the plan and ask if any of them might be interested. Although only two people say yes, Ben is convinced he'll be able to come up with enough capital to start.

What would be the best legal business form for him? _____

Your Business Form

What legal form will work best for your new business? In the space below, write down your answer; then list your reasons for making the choice.

_____

_____

_____

_____

It is important to choose a legal form that will work for you and your business. Talk to an accountant, who can review your personal financial situation and your vision for your business, before you make a final decision.

Insuring Your Success

There are some businesses that obviously need insurance—a moving company, a childcare business, or a tavern, for instance. But what about the wedding photographer, a hair stylist, or a dry cleaning business? We live in a litigious society so it's possible for a business to be sued for services that don't meet the expectations of the customer: a bride who is not pleased with her wedding pictures, a customer whose hair color was not what she had envisioned, or a businessman who is upset that the dry cleaners ruined his favorite pants.

As you start your business, you must consider areas for which you need insurance coverage. You don't want to insure things unnecessarily, but you also don't want to take unreasonable chances with your business.

Types of Insurance

- **Homeowner's or renter's insurance** protects your home and furnishings and often includes several types of protection, including fire, theft, and damage. If you plan to run your business from your home, be sure to find out if the coverage applies when your residence is used for business purposes.

- **Fire insurance** protects solely against fire. This may be covered by your homeowner's policy. Again, you should check to see if having a business in your home changes the coverage in any way.

- **Liability insurance** protects you against claims from people who are injured as a result of dealing with you or your business.

- **Automobile insurance** obviously covers your car. Make sure to buy liability insurance that covers injury to employees or other parties. Your current policy probably will be affected by business use.

- **Workers' compensation insurance** is something you must have if you have employees. It protects you and your employees in case someone is injured on the job.

- **Business interruption insurance** protects you if your business is forced to close unexpectedly—because of a fire or a natural disaster, for example.

- **Key person insurance** protects you from the loss of key personnel.

- **Crime insurance** protects you from outside crime, such as vandalism, break-ins, or robberies. If your business is in your home, check your homeowner's/renter's insurance—it may not cover anything related to the business.

- **A blanket dishonesty bond** protects you from loss from dishonest employees.

- **Glass insurance** protects you from the expense of replacing broken windows.

- **Computer insurance** covers the cost of replacing your computer(s) in case of fire, theft, or accidents. (You should always keep a backup of your data!)

- **Rent insurance** guarantees payment of your rent, even if your business income is interrupted by damage from natural disasters or fire.

- **Employee benefits coverage** is unusual for a micro-business to provide. Usually a business must employ several people before this kind of insurance is affordable. Examples of employee benefit insurance policies include group life, group health, dental, and disability.

You should be aware of other alternatives to purchasing insurance. Some of the alternatives may be acceptable for your business.

- **Loss prevention programs** include wellness programs, safety procedures, training, and equipment such as burglar alarms and smoke detectors.

- **Transfer of risk** is exemplified by leasing vehicles from a company that would carry the insurance, hiring employees through temporary agencies, or drop shipping rather than storing inventory.

- **Self-insurance** is when you put money aside to cover possible losses.

Steps for Insurance Planning

1. **Evaluate the risks.** Think through where your business is at risk. What losses could your business not afford to cover without insurance?

2. **Set your priorities.** There will be some kinds of insurance you cannot afford to buy and others you can't afford *not* to buy. First, buy insurance for whatever could cause you the greatest loss. Remember, if you are the sole owner or a partner, anything you own personally can be taken to cover your business debts. The chance of a loss might be small, but it might be a chance you can't afford to take. Decide which kinds of insurance you must have. List other kinds of insurance you would like to have. Decide which is most important.

3. **Make a plan.** Write down what insurance you need and what you want it to do for you.

4. **Find an agent.** Make sure the agent is someone you can trust. If possible, ask friends for agents they trust. Your insurance agent is a professional you are hiring. Interview them and ask for references just as you would when hiring any professional.

5. **Be economical.** Work with your agent to find the policy that is best for you. There are a number of ways you can get more insurance for your money, including these:

   - Compare prices between companies. (Be sure you are comparing prices for the same coverage.)

   - Carry as high a deductible as you can afford.

   - Avoid buying insurance for something already covered in another policy. Buy package plans if they fit what you need.

   - Buy very specific policies if you don't need more general coverage. (For example, don't pay big bucks for a renter's policy if all you want to cover is your computer.)

6. **Keep good records.** Keep complete records of all policies, including type of coverage, name of insurer, dates the coverage is effective, annual premiums, claims for losses, and amounts received. Make sure to review your coverage at least once a year. And any time there are changes that might affect your coverage, let your agent know immediately.

7. **Get expert advice.** Consult an insurance specialist who isn't trying to sell you a policy. This is an area of business for which everyone should seek expert advice.

> *Be sure you have a solid insurance plan, because you have everything to lose if you don't.*

Choose the Right Insurance

Now read the following case studies and decide which type(s) of insurance each of these businesses *must have* and what other type(s) of insurance they should consider.

Sam's Sod Design

Sam runs a landscaping business. He has a truck and several pieces of motorized equipment. He is the sole owner of the business, but he often employs people to help with jobs. Almost all of the work is done at job sites, but he does rent a garage to store his equipment.

Kendra's Christmas Cuties

Kendra makes hand-decorated Christmas stockings. She and a friend work out of her house. She has a couple of sewing machines and an embroidering machine. Kendra builds up stock from January through August, which she stores in her attic. She begins making deliveries of the stockings to stores early in September.

Parker's Painting

Parker is a house painter. He has an old truck, some ladders, scaffolding, and his tools. Sometimes he does jobs alone; other times, he hires one or two people to work with him. All of his work is done at the homes of his customers. If he needs to do a lot of work to prepare the walls and windows, he sets up a scaffold.

Wendy's Wordplay

Wendy is a self-employed writer. She works out of her home and has no employees. The only equipment she uses is her computer and printer, which she bought with a loan from her credit union.

Carly's Cooking

Carly runs a catering business. She and the people she hires do all of the cooking and serving. She has a small store with a large window which she uses for displays. She also teaches a cooking class in the window so people passing by can watch. In the back of the store she has a nicely equipped kitchen with commercial equipment.

Your Insurance Priorities

Take a few minutes to review the different kinds of insurance available to small businesses. Then, in the space below, write down which types you must have for your business.

_____

_____

_____

Which other kinds of insurance would be valuable if you felt you could afford them? Circle the one(s) you think are most important.

_____

_____

_____

Summing Up

Take time to decide the best form of business for you. But don't panic if you've already started selling your product or service. If you have started as a Sole Proprietorship, you can always change your choice of business form later. Once you are aware of your insurance needs, you should also seek out an insurance agent who will give you a good price on a policy that makes the best sense for your business.

In the next chapter we look at another practical aspect of business management: managing your records (and no, we don't mean the kind you listen to).

CHAPTER 9

Managing Your Records

A well-designed system allows you to access vital information in a quick and timely manner. It's a must for your business. In this chapter, we review common record-keeping terms, outline how paperwork flows through a typical small business, and design a system based on that paperwork flow. Finally, at the end of the chapter you can find important IRS guidelines for maintaining your records.

Keep Your Records Well

If your business is to succeed, you need a system for recording facts and maintaining records that document your daily operations. A good record-keeping system will help you discover whether your business is operating at a profit or a loss, keep track of when to pay your bills, know when and how much customers owe you, monitor your bank balances, aid you in tax preparation, and much more.

If your system is easy to use, you are more likely to maintain it consistently. The more complicated or cumbersome the design, the more apt you are to neglect your record-keeping. Here are some guidelines for effective record-keeping.

Guidelines for Record-Keeping

- Find an accountant with whom you are comfortable and create your system according to his or her directions.
- Make your system simple and maintain it regularly.
- Record business transactions only. Personal transactions must be separate from your business.
- Open a business checking account and use the check register to document all of your *receipts* (money coming in) and *disbursements* (money going out). Write checks to avoid making cash purchases.
- Save receipts to document all your business expenses.
- Make copies of all invoices and sales receipts issued by your business.
- Keep your business records for as long as the IRS recommends (usually three or four years, depending on the type of record).
- Store your old records in one place. Mark records according to year and record type.
- When you are in doubt about whether to keep a receipt or record a transaction, do it anyway! Ask your accountant later whether it is correct.

Information Is a Management Tool

Some business owners simply deliver a box stuffed with assorted documents to their accountants at the end of the year. They pay their accountants to read, sort, and interpret these documents, work they can easily perform themselves. Only at this point, after the fact, do they receive financial reports that tell them whether their businesses are succeeding or failing. These owners manage their businesses in the dark, without the benefit of timely financial information.

When you create and maintain a simple record-keeping system, you will always have the information you need at your fingertips. And make no mistake: You do need this information to manage your business wisely.

Don't drop all of your receipts and bills into a pile with the intention of getting to them later. The longer you wait, the more monumental the task becomes and the less likely you are to undertake it. It takes little effort to handle your documents correctly *as you receive them,* and it will save you a great deal of time, money, and aggravation in the long run.

Common Record-Keeping Terms

Before you learn how to manage your records, there are several terms you should be familiar with:

- **Accounts payable/Trade payable:** Money you owe to your regular business creditors. Unpaid amounts are **open accounts payable.** After they have been paid, they are **closed accounts payable.**

- **Accounts receivable/Trade receivable:** Money owed to you by your customers. Unpaid amounts are **open accounts receivable.** After they have been paid, they are **closed accounts receivable.**

- **Cash sales:** Sales made to customers when no credit has been extended. Cash sales are paid for at the time the sale is made and are documented with a **cash sale receipt.**

- **Cash receipts:** Any receipt of money. A cash receipt occurs both when a customer pays your accounts receivable (credit was extended) and when a customer pays a cash sale (no credit was extended). The term can be misleading, because it can represent cash, checks, and credit card sales.

- **Credit memo:** A reduction or credit applied against a previously issued invoice. Credit memos can be a result of shipping errors, price reductions, damaged goods, returns, or canceled orders. Credit memos have unique identifying numbers.

- **Debit memo:** An increase or debit applied against a previously issued invoice. Debit memos can be a result of original invoice errors, price adjustments, or order add-ons. Debit memos have unique identifying numbers.

- **Invoice:** A bill sent from a creditor to a customer. Invoices have payment terms consistent with the type of account the customer has with the creditor. Invoices have unique identifying numbers.

- **Invoice terms:** The payment agreement a creditor extends to a customer. Common invoice terms include these:
  - **COD:** Cash on delivery.
  - **Due upon receipt:** Payment due upon receipt of invoice.

- Net 10, Net 15, Net 30: The number of days (10, 15, 30, etc.) before payment in full is due.

  ○ 2/10 Net/30: 2 percent discount can be taken if paid within 10 days, or full payment is due in 30 days.

- **Packing slip:** The document a business encloses with a shipment to a customer. The packing slip verifies the contents of the shipment and compares it to the customer's order. Packing slips reference the customer's purchase order number, if applicable, and contain all relevant shipping information. Packing slips have unique identifying numbers.

- **Purchase order:** The form a business uses to place an order with a creditor. Purchase orders (POs) specify the buyer's name, account number, billing address, shipping address, and order details. POs have unique identifying numbers.

It's Not Personal, It's Only Business

The first rule of record keeping for your business is that personal and business transactions must be kept separate. In order to keep your funds separate, it is important that you open a business checking account. Call your local bank and ask what their requirements are to open a business checking account. They will likely require a minimum deposit amount, and most banks require that you have an Employer Identification Number (EIN), also known as a Federal Tax Identification Number (FTIN), in order to open a business account.

The EIN is a nine-digit number assigned by the Internal Revenue Service (IRS) used to identify a business. EINs are used by employers, sole proprietors, corporations, partnerships, non-profit organizations, and other business entities. An EIN can be obtained from the IRS by submitting a completed SS4 form either online (where you can get your number in just a few minutes), by mail, via fax, or by calling the toll-free number at (800) 829-4933. For more information about obtaining an EIN, visit the IRS Web site at www.irs.gov/businesses/small/. Your accounting professional can also assist you in completing your SS4 form.

Don't Be Fooled

There is *no charge* to obtain an EIN number from the IRS. There are a number of Internet businesses that offer to process your EIN application for a fee. Some of these companies will charge your credit card and then simply direct you to the online application at the IRS Web site. Do not pay a fee for something you can access for free.

Once you have opened your business checking account, keep the following in mind:

- Pay ALL of your business expenses through your business checking account (never from personal accounts).

- Pay ALL of your personal expenses from your personal resources (never from your business accounts).

- DO NOT co-mingle funds! Co-mingling means using business resources for the owner's personal purposes, or using the owner's personal resources to pay business expenses.

There may be times when a business expense is due and there isn't enough money in the business checking account to pay the expense. Say, for example, that the business telephone bill of $75 is due but there isn't enough money in the business account to pay it. The owner should NOT pay the business telephone bill with a personal check. Instead the owner should deposit sufficient personal funds into the business checking account (called an *owner's contribution to the business*) and then write a business check to pay the business phone bill.

Conversely, there may be times when the business owner needs to pay a personal expense—a daycare bill, for example—but she doesn't have sufficient funds in her personal account. She does, however, have the funds in her business account. The correct way to handle this situation is for the owner to issue herself a paycheck from the business account, which the business records as salary expense. The check is then deposited into the owner's personal account and the daycare bill is paid with a personal check. Make sure that the amount of the paycheck does not equal the *exact* amount as the personal bill to be paid. Also, the business should have a history of issuing the owner regular paychecks.

Taking the added steps to avoid co-mingling may seem inconvenient, but there is more at stake here than just following proper accounting procedures. When a business owner establishes a formal business entity, such as a corporation or a limited liability company (see chapter 8), the owner is essentially saying that she and the business are separate legal entities and she has no personal liability for the debts of the business. As long as the owner respects this "separateness," the owner remains liable only for her own personal debts and the business remains liable for the debts of the business.

But if the business owner does not respect this separateness—if she co-mingles personal and business funds, for example—the owner risks having her creditors "pierce the corporate veil," proving that the business owner didn't operate the business as a separate entity. The result can be that the owner may have unlimited liability for the debts of the business.

A Simple System

The first step in creating a simple record-keeping system is to establish a way to manage the paperwork your business generates and receives. This might include bills, receipts for expenses, bank statements, cash register tapes, and invoices you send to customers. The second step is to record all of your business transactions. This chapter will introduce you to a simple method of recording transactions and managing your paperwork using supplies you can purchase at any office supply store.

Managing the Paperwork

Managing the paperwork in your business doesn't have to be a cumbersome task. One system for doing this involves using accordion (also called "expanding") file folders that can be purchased at most office supply stores. Accordion file folders are multi-pocket folders that come in different styles. This system calls for four accordion folders to handle the daily paperwork your business receives and generates (see figure 1):

- One 31-pocket (daily) folder, with individual pockets marked 1–31. This folder will be used to manage your daily transactions for the current month. Make a label for this folder and call it **CURRENT MONTH**.

- One 12-pocket (monthly) folder, with individual pockets marked January–December. This folder is where you will temporarily place documents related to a future month. Label this folder **FUTURE MONTHS.**

- Two 26-pocket (alphabetical) folders, with individual pockets marked A–Z. These are where you will file vendor bills (in one accordion folder) and customer invoices (in the other accordion folder) alphabetically, once they have been paid. Label one of these folders **PAID CUSTOMER INVOICES** and the other **PAID VENDOR BILLS.**

Figure 1

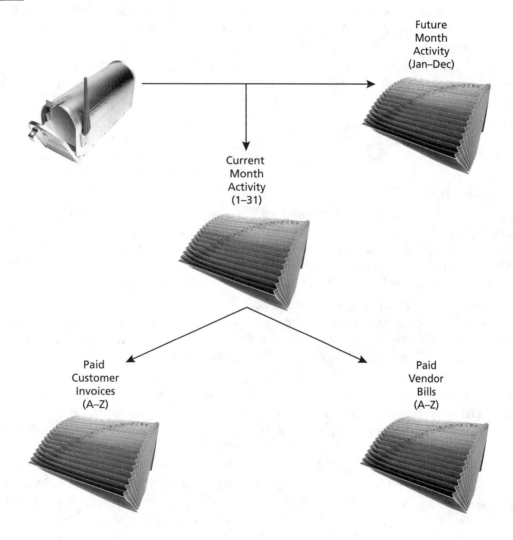

Future
Month
Activity
(Jan–Dec)

Current
Month
Activity
(1–31)

Paid
Customer
Invoices
(A–Z)

Paid
Vendor
Bills
(A–Z)

This system revolves around managing business documents on a daily basis. There are two things you must do each day to maintain this system:

- Check your incoming mail to see what new business documents (bills from supplier, utility bills, checks from customer, etc.) have arrived and immediately file these in the appropriate pocket of the appropriate file folder.

- Look in the **CURRENT MONTH** file folder, checking the pocket that corresponds to the date to see what documents require your attention that day.

Let's walk through a typical month to see how the system works.

February 1 Since today is the first day of the month, look in the **FUTURE MONTH** file folder, in the pocket marked February. Documents that were generated or received in previous months but need to be processed in February can be found here. There is only one document in the February pocket: a gas bill received the last week of January with a due date of February 15. The check must be mailed to the gas company on February 11 so that the payment will arrive on time. Move this bill to the **CURRENT MONTH** folder and file it in the pocket marked **11**.

Next, open the incoming mail and discover a business telephone bill, due on the February 25th. In order for the phone company to receive your payment on time, the check will need to be mailed no later than February 20th. In the **CURRENT MONTH** folder, place the bill in the pocket marked **20**. There are no other bills or checks in today's mail.

Finally, in the **CURRENT MONTH** folder, check the pocket labeled **1** to see if there is anything that requires attention. The pocket is empty so the document mangement tasks are complete for today.

February 3 Create an invoice for a customer, Mr. Smythe, for work now completed. You've agreed to give Mr. Smythe 15 days to pay this invoice which means his payment will be due on February 18th. Mail one copy of the invoice to Mr. Smythe and keep a file copy for yourself. Place your copy in the **CURRENT MONTH** file folder in the pocket marked **18**.

February 9 Check the incoming mail and find an invoice from a vendor, The Superior Stuff Company, for inventory delivered yesterday. The invoice is due on March 8. You plan to mail a payment to Superior Stuff on March 4 so that the check will arrive by the due date. Since this transaction will occur in a future month, file this invoice in the **FUTURE MONTH** file folder in the **March** pocket.

February 11 On this day, there is no incoming mail. Look in the pocket marked **11**; the gas bill must be paid today. Write a check to the gas company and mail it. On the gas bill, record today's date, your check number, and the amount paid. Move this paid gas bill to the **PAID VENDOR INVOICES** file folder and file it in the pocket marked **G** (for Geewhiz Gas Company).

February 18 There are no bills or checks in today's mail. Look in the **CURRENT MONTH** folder in the pocket marked **18**. There is the file copy of the invoice sent to Mr. Smythe earlier this month. You should have received his payment today but didn't. Call Mr. Smythe and ask about the status of his payment. He tells you that he mailed the check yesterday and that you should receive it within the next couple of days. Thank him and move the copy of his invoice to tomorrow's pocket, marked **19**.

February 19 Mr. Smythe's check has arrived in the mail. Pull the file copy of his invoice from the pocket marked **19**. On the file copy, record the date, the amount, and the check number of Mr. Smythe's check. Next, move the copy of his paid invoice to the **PAID CUSTOMER INVOICES** folder and file it in the pocket marked **S** (for Smythe).

February 20 There are no bills or checks in the mail, so there is nothing to be filed today. However, when you look in the pocket labeled **20**, you find the telephone bill that must be paid. Write a check and drop it in the mail. As always, record the date, your check number, and the amount paid on your file copy of the phone bill and file the paid bill alphabetically in the **PAID VENDOR BILLS** folder.

February 28 There are no bills or checks in the mail and the pocket for February 28th is empty (check the pockets for the 29th through the 31st, just in case). Look in the **FUTURE MONTHS** folder in the **March** pocket. Pull out any March documents and file them in the **CURRENT MONTH** folder under the appropriate date. You are now ready to use the system for another month.

Your business might have other documents, such as bank statements and cash register tapes. Label a separate file folder for bank statements. Once you've reconciled a statement, simply file it chronologically. Also label a folder for cash register tapes. Once you've verified that they match your daily deposit, file those as well.

As you use this system, keep an eye on the calendar and be sure to pay attention to dates that fall on weekends. Don't let documents fall through the cracks if their due dates fall on a Saturday or Sunday; file them under the dates for the previous Friday or the following Monday.

By using this simple system, you can accomplish a number of things. First, with an investment of just a few minutes each day, you can stay organized because you will manage all of your business documents as soon as you receive or generate them. There will be no mountain of paperwork taunting you and no shoe box of receipts to present to your accountant at the end of the year.

Second, by checking your **CURRENT MONTH** pockets on a daily basis, you always know when vendor bills need to be paid and when customer payments are due. Paying your bills in a timely manner can help you establish good credit history for your business (and keep your utilities from being disconnected). Staying on top of the money your customers owe you is essential to maintain positive cash flow (see Chapter 7). Remember, if you can't pay a vendor bill or you don't receive a customer payment on time, follow up as necessary with the vendor or customer and move the document to the next day's pocket so you don't forget about it.

Third, by filing all paid vendor bills and customer invoices alphabetically in their respective **PAID** folders, at the end of the year you will find all of your documents neatly gathered in one place. This can be especially convenient when you and your accountant prepare to file your annual taxes.

Finally, you can simply write the year on each of the **PAID** accordion folders, tape them shut, and you have an organized way to store your business documents should you need to access them in the future.

Recording Transactions

In addition to managing the paperwork, you must record your transactions, and you must do so daily to keep the task from becoming unwieldy. Businesses use *journals* to record financial transactions. Journals document events in chronological order. When a transaction has been recorded in a journal, it has been *posted*.

In this section you'll learn how to set up a *cash receipt and disbursement journal*. This is

Journals should be delivered to an accountant for periodic review. The accountant can then generate financial reports quickly, which saves the business owner a great deal of money in accounting fees, since the accountant works from the journal instead of from boxes of paperwork.

a simple journal meant to record all of the money coming into and going out of your business in one place. This kind of journal can be used by many small businesses.

Manual journals can be created using columnar pads (available in most office supply stores—see the example below). If a business owns a personal computer, many computerized accounting packages are available that make record-keeping easy. Journals also can be created on personal computers by using spreadsheet programs, such as Microsoft Excel.

On the following pages you will find exercises showing you how to use a simple cash journal.

Columnar Pads

This is an example of a four-column columnar pad. These pads are available with 2 to 24 (or more) "currency" columns per page.

The column on the far left is used to enter the transaction date. The wide column is used to describe the transaction. The four currency columns on the right are marked so the user can easily enter dollars and cents.

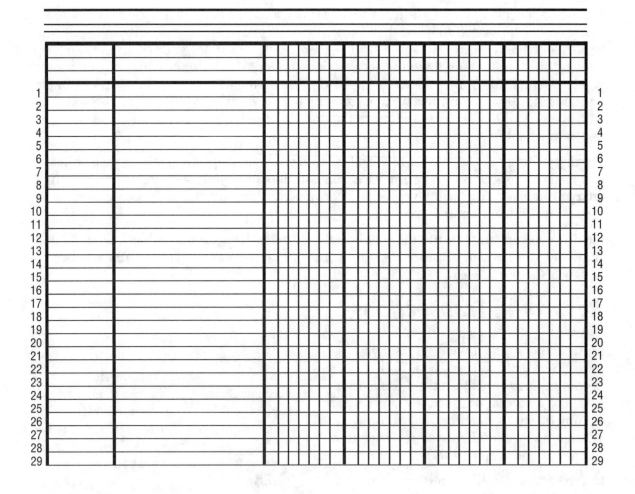

Exercise #1

In accounting, every transaction has at least two sides: one entry balanced with an equal and opposite entry. For example, when you pay the rent, you aren't just paying the rent, you take or "disburse" money from the bank to pay the rent. To record the transaction, you post one entry to the bank account and another entry to the rent expense account. Here are some examples of two sides of transactions:

	Post Entry #1 to:	Post Entry #2 to:
1. Pay rent	Bank Account ($ disbursed)	Rent Expense (expense posted)
2. Make a cash sale	Bank Account ($ deposited)	Sales Income (sale posted)
3. Pay owner's salary	Bank Account ($ disbursed)	Salary Expense (expense posted)
4. Receive a business loan	Bank Account ($ deposited)	Loan Payable (loan posted)

A business owner creates a chart of accounts to identify and number the accounts used in his or her accounting system. Based on the following chart of accounts, see if you can identify the "missing side" of each business transaction below.

Chart of Accounts

101 Checking Account
400 Sales Income
401 Misc. Income
500 Accounting
502 Automobile Expenses
505 Dues & Subscriptions
508 Depreciation
510 Fees: Bank Charges & Misc.
515 Insurance: Business
516 Insurance: Health
520 Interest Expense
525 Labor: Payroll Expense
526 Labor: Employee Benefits
530 Materials
545 Miscellaneous
550 Owner's Compensation
560 Repair & Maintenance
570 Taxes
580 Utilities

1. Employee health insurance premiums are paid.

   Entry 1: _____

   Entry 2: **516, Insurance: Health** (expense posted)

2. Gasoline expenses are reimbursed to employees.

   Entry 1: **101, Checking Account** ($ disbursed)

   Entry 2: _____

3. A customer pays cash for a purchase.

   Entry 1: **101, Checking Account** ($ deposited)

   Entry 2: _____

4. The gas bill is paid.

   Entry 1: **101, Checking Account** ($ disbursed)

   Entry 2: _____

5. The bank deducts a monthly fee directly from the checking account.

   Entry 1: _____

   Entry 2: **510, Fees: Bank Charges & Misc.** (expense posted)

Answers:
#1 Entry 1: **101 Checking Account** ($ disbursed)
#2 Entry 2: **502 Automobile Expenses** (expense posted)
#3 Entry 2: **400 Sales Income** (income posted)
#4 Entry 2: **580 Utilities** (expense posted)
#5 Entry 1: **101 Checking Account** ($ disbursed)

The Cash Receipt and Disbursement Journal

The simplest journal to keep is a cash receipt and disbursement journal. Entries posted to this journal are based on the movement of cash in and out of the business checking account. The checkbook register is the primary source of information for a cash journal.

In the example that follows from the Leaf It To Me Landscaping company, column 1 is used to record transaction dates. Column 2 is used to describe each transaction. Column 3 is to record check numbers. Columns 4 and 5 are for the *Bank Account Cash In* and *Cash Out*. Sales income is recorded in column 6. Cash in from other sources is recorded in column 7. The remaining columns (8 through 14) are for commonly used operating expenses (your business will have different headings for the expense categories based on your most frequently used operating expenses). The last two columns are for any other cash out transactions that don't occur often enough to require their own column.

On the first line of the journal, record the month's beginning bank balance. If the amount if positive, record it in column 4 (Cash In). If it is negative (let's hope it isn't), record it in column 5 (Cash Out).

Each time a deposit is made into the business checking account, it is recorded in the *Bank Account Cash In,* column 4. If the source of the deposit is a sale, the sale amount is recorded in the *Sales Income,* column 6. If the deposit comes from another source, such as loan proceeds or an owner's investment, it is recorded in column 7.

When a check is written, it is posted in *Bank Account Cash Out,* column 5. A corresponding entry is made in the appropriate expense account columns. For less common expense categories that don't have their own column, the expense account is identified in column 15 and the amount is recorded in column 16.

At the end of the month, the columns are totaled.

1. To get the ending cash balance, start with the beginning bank balance (line 1), add the total cash in, and then subtract the total cash out. This balance should agree with the checkbook register.

2. To determine whether a profit was made or a loss sustained, subtract *Total Expenses* (the sum of columns 8 through 16) from *Total Income* (column 6).

3. To double-check your numbers, start with your beginning bank balance, add or subtract your profit or loss, add any other cash in, and total. This amount should equal your ending cash balance. If it doesn't, check your math.

Using this method, you can quickly see how much sales income you've generated. It's also easy to identify how much money is being spent in each category. At the end of the year, you can total all of your monthly journals to arrive at your annual profit or loss.

You also should have created cash flow projections at the beginning of the month (review Chapter 7 for how to predict cash flow); compare these actual numbers to your projections. Is the amount of sales income as high as or higher than projected for the month? By providing historical data, cash journal totals can be used to improve future cash-flow projections.

Leaf It to Me Landscaping
Cash Receipt and Disbursement Journal

1	2	3	4	5	6	7	8	9	10	11	12	13	14	15	16
												Expenses			
			Bank Account		Sales	Other		Flowers	Gasoline		Top	Sub-Contract	Owner's	General Accounts	
Year:	200X														
Month:	July	Check #	Cash In	Cash Out	Income	Cash In	Chemicals	& Plants	(for equip)	Mulch	Soil	Labor	Comp.	Desc.	Amount
Date	Description														
	Beginning Bank Bal		$ 1,327.82												
7/1	The Mulch Man	145		$ 75.00						$ 75.00					
7/2	Carter's Greenhouse	146		$ 125.00				$ 125.00							
7/2	Mr. Johnson		$975.00		$ 975.00										
7/7	Visa Credit Card	147		$ 119.98			$ 12.95		$ 15.92					truck maint	$ 91.11
7/10	Jackie Hoover	148		$ 200.00								$ 200.00			
7/13	Mr. Clinton		750.00		$ 750.00										
7/13	Green thumb	149		$ 75.00							$ 75.00				
7/18	Mrs. Kennedy		500.00		$ 500.00										
7/21	Office Supply Store	150		$ 48.00										office supplies	$ 48.00
7/22	Mrs. Ford		1,200.00		$ 1,200.00										
7/29	Sally Owens	151		$ 2,200.00									$ 2,200.00		
	Monthly Totals		$ 3,425.00	$ 2,842.98	$ 3,425.00	$ -	$ 12.95	$ 125.00	$ 15.92	$ 75.00	$ 75.00	$ 200.00	$ 2,200.00	$ -	$ 139.11
	Ending Bank Bal		$ 1,909.84												

$ 2,842.98

Total Sales Income (column 6) $ 3,425.00

Total Expenses (add columns 8–16) $ 2,842.98

Profit or Loss $ 582.02

Beginning Bank Bal $ 1,327.82

+/- Profit (Loss) $ 582.02

+ Other Cash In $ -

Ending Cash Balance $ 1,909.84

Journaling Activity

Post the following August transactions for Leaf It to Me Landscaping on the blank cash receipts and disbursements journal found on page 115. After posting the daily transactions, total your columns, calculate the ending bank balance, and discover whether this small business realized a profit or loss for the month. You can check your journal against the completed journal on page 116.

Post the following August transactions:

Date	Transaction
—	Bring the July ending bank balance forward and record it on line 1 as the beginning bank balance for August.
3	Purchase mulch from The Mulch Man: check #152, $75.
10	Receive payment of $1,200 from customer Mrs. Bush.
13	Pay sub-contract Jackie Hoover: check #153, $300.
17	Pay Visa credit card: check #154, $200 for chemicals ($25), plants & flowers ($150), gasoline ($20), and office supplies ($5).
21	Receive payment of $1,000 from customer Mrs. Carter.
22	Purchase top soil from Green Thumb: check #155, $90.
24	Pay Al's Autos for truck maintenance: check #156, $30.
27	Pay Sally Owens owner's compensation: check #157, $1,500.

Use your completed journal to answer the following questions:

1. What was Sally's beginning bank balance? $ _____

2. What was her ending bank balance? $ _____

3. How much sales income did Sally make in August? $ _____

4. How much were her expenses? $ _____

5. How much did she pay herself in August? $ _____

6. Did she have a profit or a loss for the month?

   What was the amount? $ _____

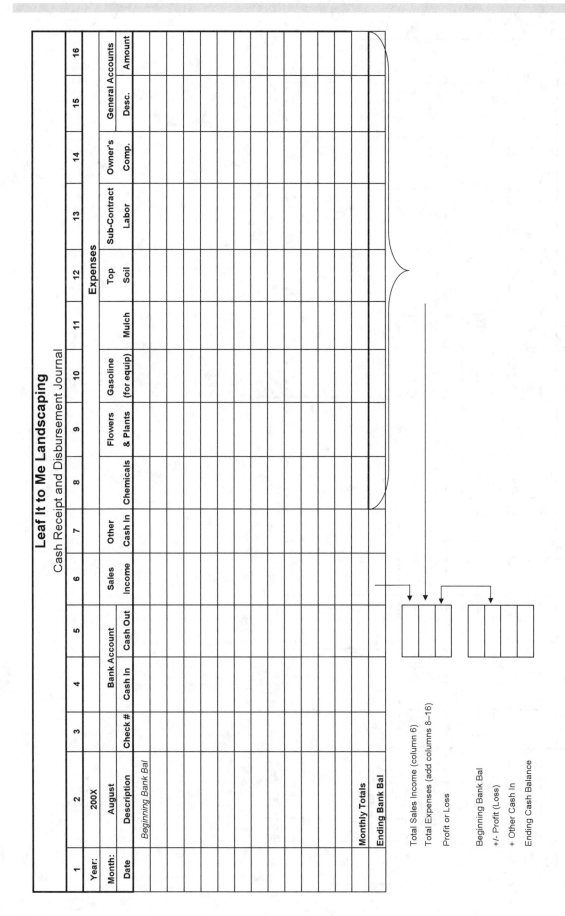

Leaf It to Me Landscaping

Cash Receipt and Disbursement Journal

1	2	3	4	5	6	7	8	9	10	11	12	13	14	15	16
Year:	**200X**														
Month:	**August**		**Bank Account**		**Sales**	**Other**						**Sub-Contract**	**Owner's**	**General Accounts**	
											Expenses				
Date	**Description**	**Check #**	**Cash In**	**Cash Out**	**Income**	**Cash In**	**Chemicals**	**Flowers & Plants**	**Gasoline (for equip)**	**Mulch**	**Top Soil**	**Labor**	**Comp.**	**Desc.**	**Amount**
	Beginning Bank Bal														
	Monthly Totals														
	Ending Bank Bal														

Total Sales Income (column 6)

Total Expenses (add columns 8–16)

Profit or Loss

Beginning Bank Bal

+/- Profit (Loss)

+ Other Cash In

Ending Cash Balance

Leaf It to Me Landscaping
Cash Receipt and Disbursement Journal

1	2	3	4	5	6	7	8	9	10	11	12	13	14	15	16
Year:	200X											Expenses			
Month:	August		Bank Account		Sales	Other	Chemicals	Flowers & Plants	Gasoline (for equip)	Mulch	Top Soil	Sub-Contract Labor	Owner's Comp.	General Accounts	
Date	Description	Check #	Cash In	Cash Out	Income	Cash In								Desc.	Amount
	Beginning Bank Bal		$ 1,909.84												
8/3	The Mulch Man	152		$ 75.00						$ 75.00					
8/10	Mrs. Bush		$ 1,200.00		$ 1,200.00										
8/13	Jackie Hoover	153		$ 300.00								$ 300.00			
8/17	Visa Credit Card	154		$ 200.00			$ 25.00	$ 150.00	$ 20.00					off supplies	$ 5.00
8/21	Mrs Carter		$ 1,000.00		$ 1,000.00										
8/22	Green Thumb	155		$ 90.00							$ 90.00				
8/24	Al's Auto's	156		$ 30.00										truck maint	$ 30.00
8/27	Sally Owens	157		$ 1,500.00									$ 1,500.00		
	Monthly Totals		$ 2,200.00	$ 2,195.00	$ 2,200.00	$ -	$ 25.00	$ 150.00	$ 20.00	$ 75.00	$ 90.00	$ 300.00	$ 1,500.00	$ -	$ 35.00
	Ending Bank Bal		$ 1,914.84												

$ 2,195.00

Total Sales Income (column 6) $ 2,200.00

Total Expenses (add columns 8–16) $ 2,195.00

Profit or Loss $ 5.00

Beginning Bank Bal $ 1,909.84

+/- Profit (Loss) $ 5.00

+ Other Cash In $ -

Ending Cash Balance $ 1,914.84

Using Accounting Software

If you own a personal computer, consider using an accounting software program to maintain your business records. One of the most popular and easy-to-use is QuickBooks, by Intuit, Inc. This software includes a built-in tutorial, step-by-step interview questions to walk you through the initial setup of your system, and an easy-to-follow Help function. Available features include accounts payables, accounts receivable, inventory, payroll, banking, job costing, time billing, and credit card processing.

Intuit also offers QuickBooks Simple Start, a bookkeeping software package designed for the very small business that only needs to track money coming in and going out of the business. This package is ideal for business owners who don't need or want to learn a more complicated accounting system.

There are many other fine products available, most at reasonable prices. Before deciding on a software package, speak to your accountant or bookkeeper to determine which software package he or she uses. The process of delivering information to your accounting professional will be simpler if you use the same or compatible software.

It is a good idea to have an accounting professional assist you when you first set up your company and begin to enter transactions on a computerized system. Although most accounting software applications are very user-friendly, they are still quite simple to mess up if you don't know what you're doing. It is helpful to understand the fundamentals of manual record-keeping (covered in this chapter) even if you plan to use a computerized system.

General Information

The following section deals with how long you should keep documents, questions you should ask when interviewing an accountant, and Internal Revenue Service publications and guidelines to be aware of.

How Long to Keep Your Records

- Keep all business records for at least three years from the date the tax return was due or filed or two years from the date the tax was paid, whichever occurs later.
- Keep asset records for at least as long as the asset is in service. Assets include things your business owns, such as equipment and furniture. If you replace an asset, you may have to keep the records of the original asset for as long as the new asset is in service. Have your accountant advise you.
- You may need to keep some records for an indefinite period to support decisions regarding changes in accounting methods or inventory valuations.
- If you are an employer, retain all records and returns pertaining to employment taxes—such as income tax withholding, Social Security taxes, and federal unemployment taxes—for at least four years after the due date of the return or four years after the date the tax was paid, whichever is later.

Refer to IRS Publication 583 for more information on how long to keep records.

Suggested IRS Publications

The following publications can be obtained through your local IRS office:

Publication Number	Title
15	Employers Tax Guide (Circular E)
17	Your Federal Income Tax
334	Tax Guide for Small Business
463	Travel, Entertainment, Gift, and Car Expense
505	Tax Withholding & Estimated Tax
525	Taxable & Nontaxable Income
535	Business Expenses
541	Tax Information on Partnerships
542	Tax Information on Corporations
560	Retirement Plans for Small Business
583	Starting a Business and Keeping Records
587	Business Use of Your Home (Including Use by Day Care Providers)

The IRS and other federal agencies provide assistance to business owners. For more information, contact your local IRS office Monday through Friday during normal business hours at the Telephone Assistance for Businesses toll-free number 1-800-829-4933.

You can also access the IRS on the Internet at www.irs.gov/businesses/small. Tax forms can be ordered through the IRS Web site, or you can receive forms and instructions by calling 1-800-829-3676. You should receive your order within 10 days.

How to Select an Accountant

When starting your business, it is a good idea to contact an accountant to help you set up your manual or automated record-keeping system. While many small business owners think this is an unnecessary expense, the truth is, paying an accountant to counsel you when you first open your business can save you substantially in the long run. Many small business owners have had to recreate their books from scratch come tax season because they didn't know what they were doing when they launched their business.

Not all accountants are created equal, however. Here is a list of questions you should ask when you are interviewing accountants:

- Can you provide me with some client references from other businesses in my field?
- How are your fees structured?
- How often will we meet?
- What can I do to reduce your workload (and thus your fees)?

- Are you qualified to discuss my business's tax requirements?
- Will you review and advise me regarding my record-keeping?
- What are your office hours?
- Is there a staff member available when you are not?
- How quickly will my financial reports be generated and delivered?
- May I have an engagement letter that details our agreement?

Employee or Independent Contractor?

According to the IRS, an employer generally must withhold income taxes, withhold and pay Social Security and Medicare taxes, and pay unemployment taxes on wages paid to an employee. An employer generally does not have to withhold or pay taxes on payments to independent contractors, however.

The general rule is that an individual is an independent contractor if you (the person for whom the services are performed) have the right to control or direct only the *result* of the work and not the *means and methods* of accomplishing the result. Under common-law rules, anyone who performs services for you is your employee if you have the right to control what will be done *and* how it will be done.

To help you determine whether an individual is an employee under the common-law rules, the IRS has identified some guidelines to determine whether sufficient control is present to establish an employer-employee relationship. If an employer makes an incorrect determination and treats an employee as an independent contractor, *the employer could be held personally liable for an amount equal to the taxes that should have been withheld.*

The following rules will help you determine whether an individual is an employee or an independent contractor.

- **Behavioral Control:** Facts that show whether the business has the right to direct and control how the worker does the task for which the worker is hired include the type and degree of
  - Instructions the business gives the worker (when and where to do the work, what tools to use, what workers to hire or assist with the work, where to purchase supplies and services, what work must be performed by a specific individual, what order or sequence to follow).
  - Training the business gives the worker. An employee may be trained to perform services in a particular manner. Independent contractors ordinarily use their own methods.

- **Financial Control:** Facts that show whether the business has a right to control the business aspects of the worker's job, including
  - The extent to which the worker has unreimbursed business expenses.
  - The extent to which the worker makes services available to the general market (other than the business in question).
  - How the business pays the worker.

For more information on differentiating between employees and independent contractors, request IRS publication 15A.

Summing Up

An effective record-keeping system is a must for your small business. A well-designed system is simple and easy to use and allows you to access important information quickly. Whether you choose to create a manual record-keeping system or use a personal computer and small business accounting software, it will be helpful to first understand the fundamentals of manual record-keeping. Consider what information you need to manage your business, what paperwork your business generates, and what documents you receive as you design your system. Don't be afraid to consult a bookkeeper or an accountant familiar with your type of business to assist you in setting up your system.

Much of your record-keeping will be used to generate financial statements, which you can then use to better manage your business. The next chapter will teach you more about financial statements and how to use them.

CHAPTER 10

Understanding Financial Statements

In this chapter, you learn to read financial statements. Successful business owners use financial reports as vital management tools. Most small businesses don't generate their own financials, but all small business owners should understand how to read them.

After you understand the components of financial statements, you'll have the chance to examine the effect different management decisions have on similar businesses. You'll also learn what lenders look for when analyzing financial reports.

Just the Facts, Ma'am

Who uses financial statements? What do they tell about a business? How often should they be generated? Most importantly, why bother? You find out in this section.

Who?

Financial statements are used by many people, but none more important than the business owner. Successful business owners use financial statements as management tools. They refer to these reports on a regular basis to make daily operating decisions. And before they make any critical business decision, they examine their financial reports.

Some business owners believe that financial statements are for accountants and bankers. They pay an accountant to generate the statements and then send copies to the bank. They rely on their accountant to read the reports and alert them to any problems. By doing this, they relinquish some control of their businesses and rely on chance (or someone else's judgement) that everything will be all right.

What?

Financial statements consist of two primary elements: the balance sheet and the income statement. When people ask for financial statements, sometimes they also want other reports, such as cash-flow statements or projections. Since we've already discussed cash flow projections in a previous chapter, we'll just examine the balance sheet and income statement in this chapter.

When?

How often financial statements should be generated and reviewed depends on the size and type of business. Some businesses need only quarterly financial reports, but most businesses are better served with monthly reports. If your record-keeping system includes an up-to-date general journal, you already have considerable financial information on a daily basis. Your accountant can help you determine what best suits your information needs.

Why?

Operating a business without financial statements is like driving a car blindfolded. You wouldn't know when (or if) you reached your destination—and that would be the least of your problems. More important, you couldn't see obstacles in your way, and you wouldn't know if you were in danger until it was too late. You couldn't see what you were doing right or where you were going off course. You could get hurt because of your recklessness, and so could others. Whether driving a car or running a business, you need to see where you've been, where you are, and where you're going.

You Ought to Be in Pictures!

Before you can use your financial statement as a management tool, you must first understand how to read it. Financial statements are pictures of your business that serve two important functions:

- The balance sheet reports the net worth of the business.
- The income statement reports how the business is being operated.

The Balance Sheet

The balance sheet is a financial snapshot of your business at a given point in time. It tells you, as of a specific date, several important things:

- What your business owns
- The debt for which your business is liable
- The net worth of your business

The information is categorized as follows:

- Assets (what you own)
- Liabilities (what you owe)
- Equity (your net worth)

Since a balance sheet is a financial picture taken on a specific date, it is labeled as such: Balance sheet for ABC Company, Inc., as of XX/XX/XXXX.

The Income Statement

Your income statement is a financial movie that covers a specific period of time. It tells you whether your business operated at a profit or suffered a loss during that time.

This information is categorized as follows:

- Income (revenue generated)
- Expenses (cost of operations)
- Profit or loss (difference between income and expenses)

Since an income statement covers a specific period, it is labeled as such: Income Statement for ABC Company, Inc., for the period ending XX/XX/XXXX.

Exercise #1

Perhaps the easiest way to understand financial statements is to examine a set. In this exercise, we identify an asset, liability, equity, income, and expense item and indicate whether each is found on the balance sheet or income statement.

Month #1	Description	Balance Sheet/ Income Statement
Mary's take-home pay from her job is $3,000 per month.	Income	Income Statement
Her living expenses total $2,500 per month.	Expenses	Income Statement
The difference between her income and expenses is $500.	Profit (Loss)	Income Statement
Mary puts her monthly "profit" into a savings account.	Asset	Balance Sheet
Mary just bought a car for $17,000.	Asset	Balance Sheet
She put $2,000 down to buy the car.	Equity	Balance Sheet
Mary has an auto loan with a balance of $15,000.	Liability	Balance Sheet
Mary is buying a house; the purchase price is $125,000.	Asset	Balance Sheet
She put $15,000 down on the house.	Equity	Balance Sheet
She has a mortgage loan balance of $110,000.	Liability	Balance Sheet

Mary's Balance Sheet as of 1/31/2XXX

Assets

Bank Balance	$500
House	$125,000
Car	$17,000
Assets:	$142,500

Total Assets:	**$142,500**

Liabilities

Mortgage loan	$110,000
Car loan	$15,000
Liabilities:	**$125,000**

Equity (net worth)

Home equity:	$15,000
Car equity:	$2,000
Profit (Loss)	$500
Equity:	**$17,500**

Total Liabilities & Equity:	**$142,500**

Mary's Income Statement as of 1/31/2XXX

Income

Salary	$3,000

Expenses

Mortgage Payment	$900
Clothing	$100
Groceries & Dining Out	$400
Utilities	$200
Homeowners Insurance	$100
Property Taxes	$150
Car Payment	$350
Gas & Maintenance	$200
Miscellaneous	$100
Total Expenses	**$2,500**
Profit (Loss)	**$500**

Is This Picture in Focus?

Take a closer look at some examples of *assets, liabilities,* and *equity:*

- David buys a car for $15,000. He puts $5,000 down and takes out a car loan for $10,000.

Asset (what you own)	Automobile	$15,000
Liability (what you owe)	Auto loan	$10,000
Equity (net worth)	Auto equity	$5,000

- Kathy buys a house for $150,000. Her down payment is $15,000. Her mortgage is $135,000.

Asset (what you own)	Home	$150,000
Liability (what you owe)	Mortgage	$135,000
Equity (net worth)	Home equity	$15,000

- James has a savings account balance of $2,000. He has credit card debt of $1,800.

Asset (what you own)	Savings account	$2,000
Liability (what you owe)	Credit card debt	$1,800
Equity (net worth)	Net worth	$200

Looking at the examples above, you will notice that there is a common equation:

$$\text{Assets} - \text{Liabilities} = \text{Equity}$$

Another way to write this same equation is as follows:

$$\text{Assets} = \text{Liabilities} + \text{Equity}$$

Assets = Liabilities + Equity is *the* fundamental accounting equation. Balance sheets are so called because they are designed to balance using this equation. Following is an example of a balance sheet.

David's Balance Sheet as of 1/31/2XXX

Assets		Liabilities	
Automobile	$15,000	Auto loan	$10,000
		Equity	
		Auto equity	$5,000
Total Assets:	$15,000	**Total Liabilities & Equity:**	$15,000

The Whole Family Album

Income statements describe operating income and expenses over a period of time (for example, one month). If a business generates more income than expense, it earns a profit. If a business incurs more expense than income, it suffers a loss.

We know that balance sheets report the net worth (equity) of a business and that income statements report profit or loss. If a business is profitable, doesn't that increase its equity? If a business is suffering a loss, doesn't that decrease its equity? If so, then doesn't the profit or loss of the income statement need to be reflected on the balance sheet?

The answer is yes. Profit or loss is taken directly from the income statement and recorded on the balance sheet in an equity account called *retained earnings.* In the following example, you can see how this happens.

ABC Widgets

ABC Widgets is owned by Mr. I.M. Good. Mr. Good started his business with an initial investment of $5,000.

Here is Mr. Good's opening balance sheet:

Balance Sheet for ABC Widgets as of 1/1/2XXX

Assets		Liabilities	
Bank account	$5,000	Accounts payable	$0
Accounts receivable	$0		
Inventory	$0	**Equity**	
Equipment	$0	Owner's equity	$5,000
		Retained earnings	$0
		Total Equity	**$5,000**
Total Assets	**$5,000**	**Liabilities & Equity**	**$5,000**

Mr. Good started his business with $5,000 of his personal savings. His investment in his business is recorded as *equity* in an account called *owner's equity.* The $5,000 balance will remain unless Mr. Good reduces or increases his investment into his business. Mr. Good deposited the cash in the *bank account.* The opening balance sheet is in balance.

Mr. Good decided to market his new business aggressively. His decision to spend money on advertising has paid off. Sales are above Mr. Good's projections, and he has made a net profit of $570. Here is Mr. Good's first income statement.

Mr. Good collected $4,700 in widget sales. That income was deposited into the bank account. He also paid $1,645 in COGS and $2,485 in fixed expenses. By the end of the month, his bank balance was $5,570. The balance sheet reflects this new bank balance.

ABC Widgets earned a profit of $570. This amount is recorded as *equity, retained earnings*.

Below is the balance sheet at the end of the month.

Income Statement for ABC Widgets for Month Ending 1/31/2XXX

Income	
Widget sales	$4,700
Total Sales	**$4,700**
Cost of Goods Sold	
Widget material	$705
Widget labor	$940
Total Cost of Goods Sold	**$1,645**
Gross Profit	**$3,055**
Fixed Expenses	
Advertising	$1,000
Automobile	$100
Bank charges	$10
Insurance	$100
Office supplies	$25
Owner's compensation	$750
Rent	$500
Total Fixed Expenses	**$2,485**
Net Profit	**$570**

Balance Sheet for ABC Widgets as of 1/31/2XXX

Assets		Liabilities	
Bank account	$5,570	Accounts payable	$0
Accounts receivable	$0		
Inventory	$0	**Equity**	
Equipment	$0	Owner's equity	$5,000
		Retained earnings	$570
		Total Equity	**$5,570**
Total Assets	**$5,570**	**Liabilities & Earnings**	**$5,570**

XYZ Gadgets

I.M. Good's Brother, Notso, started a business the same month: XYZ Gadgets. Notso also started with a $5,000 investment. Notso's opening balance sheet for XYZ was identical to ABC's balance sheet.

Notso made some different management decisions. He spent very little time and money marketing his new business. As a result, his sales are less than he had hoped for. He had to pay high prices for materials because he didn't take advantage of volume discounts. His labor costs were high because he didn't hire experienced employees; the inexperienced staff was slow in producing gadgets. Notso didn't pay himself a salary. He ended the month with a $10 loss.

During the month, Notso collected $1,500 in cash sales and paid $675 in COGS and $835 in fixed expenses. His ending bank balance was $4,990.

Notso posted a loss of $10 to retained earnings.

I.M. and Notso started their businesses on the same day with the same amount of money. In one month, ABC was earning a profit, but XYZ was suffering a loss. Is XYZ worth less than ABC?

Income Statement for XYZ Gadgets for Month Ending 1/31/2XXX

Income	
Gadget sales	$1,500
Total Sales	**$1,500**
Cost of Goods Sold	
Gadget material	$300
Gadget labor	$375
Total Cost of Goods Sold	**$675**
Gross Profit	**$825**
Fixed Expenses	
Advertising	$100
Automobile	$100
Bank charges	$10
Insurance	$100
Office supplies	$25
Owner's compensation	$0
Rent	$500
Total Fixed Expenses	**$835**
Net Profit	**($10)**

Balance Sheet for XYZ Gadgets as of 1/31/2XXX

Assets		Liabilities	
Bank account	$4,990	Accounts payable	$0
Accounts receivable	$0		
Inventory	$0	**Equity**	
Equipment	$0	Owner's equity	$5,000
		Retained earnings:	($10)
		Total Equity	**$4,990**
Total Assets	**$4,990**	**Liabilities & Equity**	**$4,990**

Cash vs. Credit

In the prior examples, ABC's transactions were all made in cash: Cash sales were deposited into the bank account, and cash expenses were paid from the bank account. Here's what that balance sheet looked like:

Balance Sheet for ABC Widgets as of 1/31/2XXX

Assets		Liabilities	
Bank account	$5,570	Accounts payable	$0
Accounts receivable	$0		
Inventory	$0	**Equity**	
Equipment	$0	Owner's equity	$5,000
		Retained earnings	$570
		Total Equity	**$5,570**
Total Assets	**$5,570**	**Liabilities & Equity**	**$5,570**

Take a look at what would happen if ABC had the *same amount of sales and expenses,* but incurred accounts receivable for some of those sales and accounts payable for some of those expenses.

- Remember, sales totaled $4,700. Assume that $4,000 was paid in cash and $700 remained in accounts receivable.
- Expenses (COGS & fixed) totaled $4,130. Assume that $3,000 was paid in cash and $1,130 remained in accounts payable.
- The bank account had $5,000 in cash at the beginning of the month. Add $4,000 in cash sales and subtract $3,000 in expenses paid. The ending bank balance is $6,000.
- The accounts receivable balance is $700. The accounts payable balance is $1,130.
- The income statement reflects no changes, and retained earnings are still $570. The new balance sheet would look like this:

Balance Sheet for ABC Widgets as of 1/31/2XXX

Assets		Liabilities	
Bank account	$6,000	Accounts payable	$1,130
Accounts receivable	$700		
Inventory	$0	**Equity**	
Equipment	$0	Owner's equity	$5,000
		Retained earnings	$570
		Total Equity	**$5,570**
Total Assets	**$6,700**	**Liabilities & Equity**	**$6,700**

The business has increased assets and increased liabilities, but the *equity* of the business did not change. Offering credit to your customers and using credit offered by your suppliers will affect when cash moves into and out of your business, but it will not affect your profit or loss or the overall value of your business.

The Chart of Accounts

In a business, transactions occur daily. For ease in identifying all of the accounts a business may use, a listing or *chart of accounts* is created. These accounts often are numbered for easy identification. If you created a personal chart of accounts, it might look like this:

Assets	Equity	Expenses
100 Bank Account	300 Home Equity	510 Mortgage Payment
110 House	310 Auto Equity	520 Food
120 Car	333 Profit (Loss)	530 Utilities
		540 Insurance
Liabilities	**Income**	550 Auto Payment
200 Home Mortgage	400 Salary Income	560 Miscellaneous
210 Auto Loan		

Companies create their own charts of accounts, relative to the way they do business. Throughout the year, they can add new accounts to their charts as necessary. An accountant or bookkeeper can help a business establish a chart of accounts that meets its needs. A simple chart of accounts follows:

Assets
100 Regular Checking Account
105 Payroll Checking Account
110 Petty Cash on Hand
115 Trade Accounts Receivable
150 Equipment
155 Furniture and Fixtures
160 Small Tools
180 Inventory on Hand
510 Fees: Bank Charges & Misc.

Liabilities
200 Trade Accounts Payable
205 Payroll Taxes Payable
210 Bank Notes Payable
250 Note Payable: Owner
530 Materials

Equity
300 Owner's Contribution
399 Retained Earnings: Year to Date
570 Taxes
580 Utilities

Income
400 Sales Income
401 Misc. Income

Expenses
500 Accounting
502 Automobile Expenses
505 Dues and Subscriptions
508 Depreciation
515 Insurance: Business
516 Insurance: Health
520 Interest Expense
525 Labor: Payroll Expense
526 Labor: Employee Benefits
545 Miscellaneous
550 Owner's Compensation
560 Repair & Maintenance

A Picture in Review

Let's review what we've learned so far. There are five types of accounts:

- Assets (what you own)
- Liabilities (what you owe)
- Equity (net worth)
- Income
- Expenses

Balance Sheet

Assets	Liabilities
	+ Equity

Assets = Liabilities + Equity

- Contains assets, liabilities, and equity
- Reports net worth as of a specific date
- Must balance
- Useful for providing an overview of a business's financial status

Income Statement

Income
− Expenses
= Net Profit (Loss)

- Contains income and expenses
- Reports operating profit or loss for a specific period of time
- Useful for measuring success over time

If a business earns a profit, equity increases.

If a business suffers a loss, equity decreases.

Profit or loss is posted to the balance sheet in an equity account called retained earnings.

Retained Earnings Accumulate

You know there is a relationship between income statements and balance sheets: Profit or loss from the income statement is posted to the balance sheet as retained earnings. In the first month of operations, profit or loss and retained earnings will be the same. Each month thereafter, the profit or loss amount from the monthly income statement is added to the prior retained earnings balance.

Exercise #2

In this exercise, you will create financial statements. Fill in the blanks; then enter the information onto the worksheet on the following page.

1. The name of your imaginary person is _____. Enter this name at the top of both the balance sheet and the income statement.

2. Your person brings home a salary of $_____ each month. Enter this amount on the income statement. If your person has other income, identify this also.

3. Your person is buying a _____. The purchase price is $_____ (asset), and it is being purchased with a down payment of $_____ (equity) and a loan for the balance of $_____ (liability). Enter these amounts on the balance sheet.

4. The monthly household expenses for your person are the following:

Housing expense	$ _____
Food	_____
Utilities	_____
Insurance	_____
Car payment	_____
Daycare	_____
_____	_____
_____	_____
_____	_____
_____	_____
_____	_____

   Enter these amounts where they belong on the income statement.

5. If you'd like, your person is also purchasing a _____. The purchase price is $_____, and it is being purchased with a down payment of $_____ and a loan for the balance of $_____. Enter these amounts on the balance sheet. If your person owns anything else or owes anything else, include these amounts, too.

6. Total your income statement and determine whether your person ends with a profit or loss. Remember to reflect this amount on the balance sheet.

7. Now total your balance sheet. Remember that *the balance sheet must balance.* If it doesn't, try to determine what is missing.

   HINT: Did your person end with a profit or loss in number 6? Where did that cash go—into a checking account? Did you remember to include a checking account on the balance sheet?

Exercise #2 Worksheet

_____

Balance Sheet as of 1/31/2XXX

Assets   Liabilities

_____ $ _____   _____ $ _____

_____ $ _____   _____ $ _____

_____ $ _____   _____ $ _____

_____ $ _____   _____ $ _____

Equity (net worth)

_____ $ _____

_____ $ _____

_____ $ _____

Total Assets $ _____   Liabilities & Equity $ _____

_____

Income Statement for Period Ending 1/31/2XXX

Income

_____ $ _____

_____ $ _____

_____ $ _____

Expenses

_____ $ _____

_____ $ _____

_____ $ _____

_____ $ _____

_____ $ _____

_____ $ _____

_____ $ _____

_____ $ _____

Profit (Loss) $ _____

Examine Your Financial Picture

The following are typical questions business owners, lenders, and accountants ask when analyzing financial statements. Keep them in mind when you review your own:

- Do assets exceed liabilities? Is there a positive or negative net worth?

- Does it appear that the values assigned to the assets are reasonable? Assets are posted at their purchase price and adjusted to market price as necessary. Have reasonable adjustments been made? Do adjustments need to be made?

- Are the assets things that can be sold quickly if necessary? What type of assets are they? How well do they hold their value?

- Do assets exceed liabilities by a large margin? If some assets had to be sold (liquidated) to pay debts, what would remain?

- Comparing income to expenses and liabilities, does it seem that money is being spent well?

- If the company suffered a sudden reduction or fluctuation in income, are there monthly expenses that could be reduced or eliminated easily?

- Are there large swings in expenses that do not correspond to swings in sales? Does it appear that the company is not controlling operating expenses?

- Do accounts receivable greatly exceed an average month of sales? If so, chances are good that receivables are not being collected in a timely manner. The older receivables become, the more difficult they are to collect.

- Do accounts payable greatly exceed an average month of operating expenses? If so, chances are good that bills are not being paid on time. This could result in suppliers no longer extending credit or delivering goods, utilities being disconnected, and loans being called.

- Are there unexplained accounts payable, such as loans or notes?

- How much money does the owner have invested in the business? How does this compare to overall debt? Is the company being operated using nothing but OPM (other people's money)?

- How much salary is the owner taking out of the business? How does this compare to the profit or loss of the business?

Summing Up

Financial statements provide entrepreneurs with essential information about their business: they reveal how a business is operating, how much cash the business has on hand, what the debts of the business are and how much money is owed to the business. They reflect the value of the business and how the business is being managed and can point to problem areas that require an owner's attention. With this much information in one place, the smart business owner will make the effort to understand financial statements and take the time to examine them regularly.

From Dream to Reality

Turning your self-employment dream into reality can be both exhilarating and a little frightening. This book was written to take some of the mystery out of the process of starting your own business.

In this book, we've looked at some of the reasons people decide to become self-employed and why some businesses fail. We've helped you define your dream and understand how to finance it. We've shown you how to set goals and create action plans to achieve them. We've given you the worksheets to price your products and services and the steps to market your business. We've provided information about legal forms of business, insurance, cash-flow management, record-keeping, and financial statements.

Each chapter for this book gives you information about a different aspect of your small business. Consider each aspect and how it applies to your business idea. As you plan your business, write down your ideas step by step. Use these notes as the basis for your business plan—your personal guide to starting your own business. (See Appendix A for an example of the form your business plan should take.) Your business plan will help keep you grounded as your dream becomes a reality. Use it to communicate your ideas to other people. As your business grows, you should review and update your business plan to accommodate changes.

Self-employment has many rewards; among them is the satisfaction of having a dream and turning it into something real. Good luck on your journey from dream to reality.

Is an E-business Right for You?

In 1886, a shipment of gold watches was sent to a Minnesota jeweler, but the jeweler had not ordered them and refused the shipment. A 23-year-old telegraph operator working for the Minneapolis and St. Louis Railway in Redwood Falls, Minnesota, obtained the shipment and used the telegraph to sell the watches to station agents along the railroad line. Within six months he netted a $5,000 profit. Confident in his ability to become a successful entrepreneur, the young man, Richard Sears, pursued his dream and eventually launched Sears, Roebuck and Company.

In essence, selling watches over the telegraph isn't too different from selling them over the Internet. In both cases the goal is to use technology to reach the right customers faster. Of course the technology has improved dramatically, but it still takes the right kind of person with a good business idea and an entrepreneurial spirit to take advantage of it. Thousands have learned to use the Internet to launch their own business and fulfill their self-employment dream. This chapter can help you decide whether an e-business is the right choice for you.

What Is an E-business?

E-business, or electronic business, is defined as doing business using automated information systems or computers. E-business commonly refers to doing business over the Internet, and more specifically, the World Wide Web (WWW), which is the most common way people access (and thus buy stuff) online. E-business uses many Internet features such as shopping carts, e-mail, and instant messaging to allow the exchange of goods, money, or information between two businesses (called Business-to-Business or B2B) or between a business and its consumers (B2C).

E-business can be (and often is) conducted by traditional "bricks-and-mortar" businesses to showcase their merchandise online. The term *bricks-and-mortar* refers to companies that have a physical presence—a location where customers can visit and physically see, touch, and buy merchandise. Bricks-and-mortar companies that also sell merchandise online are sometimes called *clicks-and-mortar* or *clicks-and-bricks* businesses. Some e-businesses have no bricks-and-mortar location; their only means of doing business is through their Web site. Amazon.com is a well-known example of an online business. These businesses are sometimes called *virtual businesses*.

The term *e-commerce* refers to generating income using electronic means. Historically, e-commerce included all forms of electronic business, such as the use of credit cards, ATM machines, fax machines, and telephone banking. Today, e-commerce commonly refers to all the Web site features an e-business needs to accept payments online, such as an electronic shopping cart.

One advantage of an online business is that with a professional-looking Web site, a small, home-based business where the owner works on a computer at her kitchen table can have the same Internet presence as an organization with hundreds of employees in an expensive office building. With no need to lease office space or invest in expensive furniture, display cases, signage, or fixtures, an entrepreneur can launch a home-based e-business with far less initial capital than a bricks-and-mortar business. But there are some things a business owner should consider before launching an e-business.

E-business Pros and Cons

Advantages	Disadvantages
• Access to world-wide markets	• Reliance on technology (can be unstable)
• Open for business 24/7	• Lose human interaction with customers
• Low start-up and operating costs	• Must maintain online security
• Can operate from home	• Must possess or hire technical expertise
• Flexible; can make frequent changes at low cost	

Defining Your E-business

Like any other new business venture, building an e-business requires an investment of time and money that doesn't always pay off. In this section we will look at factors to consider before deciding whether an e-business is right for you.

What Are You Selling?

If you are considering launching a Web site for your business, begin by determining what you hope to accomplish by having an online presence. For example, if you are a service provider such as a roofer or a dry cleaner, having a Web site may be a valuable marketing tool to generate interest in your business. People could visit your Web site to learn about your company, read client testimonials, see your fee schedule, and get directions to your location. But very little e-commerce will take place from the Web site, as your business will not sell anything online (while powerful, computers still can't fix a roof or do laundry). Be sure you have a clear vision of what you want to accomplish by taking your business online. Complete the Web Site Planning Worksheet on page 147 to help clarify your vision.

If you hope to generate online revenue through your Web site, you must have something marketable to sell. So what, exactly, do people sell on the Internet? Let's look at three categories of online sales: products, information, and services.

Products for Sale: Everything *and* the Kitchen Sink

Almost anything you can think of can be purchased online, including the kitchen sink. From automobiles to art supplies, laptops to lobsters, movie tickets to motorcycles, consumers can buy a wide variety of products from the comfort of their home and have their purchases delivered right to their front door. It is estimated that well over a hundred million people shop online.

How do you decide which products to sell online? Consider your own hobbies, interests, and experience when deciding what to sell. Think about selling products you are knowledgeable about, because you may have to provide customer service or instructions for installation or operation.

Choose products that are in high demand and can be priced to generate a profit. Unique items such as handcrafted jewelry or private-label garments provide an opportunity to sell one-of-a-kind goods to niche markets that might best be reached online. Items that benefit a social cause, such as fair trade goods, appeal to buyers who wish to make a social statement or benefit society through their purchases. Consider selling consumable goods that need to be replaced on a regular basis—such as office supplies, cosmetics, or pet supplies—creating opportunities for recurring sales.

Avoid selling "hard sell" products online. While it may not be difficult to sell T-shirts online, swim suits and evening gowns will be harder sells because most people prefer

Products Purchased Online by U.S. Internet Users in 2005 (% of respondents)

Books	68%
Travel	67%
Music/DVDs	66%
Clothes	63%
Tickets for entertainment	54%
Electronics	52%
Toys/games	46%
Office supplies/stationery	44%
Home décor	42%
Home furnishings	36%
Photo/supplies	35%
Cosmetics	34%
Jewelry/watches	31%
Perfume/fragrance	23%
Prescriptions	23%
Pet supplies	21%
Greeting cards	18%
Groceries	12%

Note: n=945
Source: WSL Strategic Retail, November 2005; ClickZ, November 2005

to try them on before buying. Products that people want to touch, smell, or taste before buying—such as that new car or that tantalizing perfume—may sell better offline than on.

Remember to Focus

E-business allows you to reach customers that you normally couldn't in a traditional business, provided you can get their attention. Focus on selling a few related items instead of trying to sell everything to everyone. You will be more effective if you target one or two related markets.

Don't forget to think about what it will take to pack and ship products to customers. Oversized products can be time consuming to package and expensive to ship. Perishable or fragile items can result in high returns or refunds. Also, if you intend to carry an inventory, make sure you have the space to store and organize your products.

Just Drop Ship It

One way to sell products through the Internet more effectively is to use a *drop ship company.* These companies allow you to order items from suppliers who will drop ship the products directly to your customer. You don't need to keep any items in inventory, you aren't responsible for packing and shipping the items, and you don't have to pay the supplier until after you've received payment from your customer. This minimizes your risk and your start-up costs.

There are many drop ship businesses on the Internet. Do your research and use a reputable drop shipper; reviews of drop ship companies are available online. Popular drop ship companies include Doba.com (www.doba.com) and WorldWide Brands (www.worldwidebrands.com).

Information for Sale: Knowledge Is Power

Some e-businesses sell information through their Web sites. Information-based products are sometimes called *digital goods* or *knowledge-based goods.* The variety of digital goods sold on the Internet is enormous. Some examples include the following:

- Articles
- E-books (electronic books)
- E-zines (electronic magazines)
- Newsletters
- Research results
- Industry statistics
- Online courses
- Blueprints and plans
- Do-it-yourself project instructions
- Recipes
- Craft patterns

Customers may pay a subscription fee to be able to access the information, pay a per-piece price for the information, or both. However the income is generated, the delivery of the information can be fairly simple if the information is in a digital format: Typically the business either e-mails it to the customer or the customer downloads it from the Web site.

There are many advantages to selling information on the Internet:

- **Production costs are low.** Information can be digitally produced with nothing more than an investment in some software plus the time it takes to research, gather, and write the information. Many companies don't produce their own material but solicit information from others who are considered experts in the field and/or who are willing to produce it cheaper.
- **Reproduction of the product is free.** It is as simple as making a copy of the file or posting the information on your Web site.
- **There is no inventory.** Digital goods are stored on your computer.
- **The customer receives the goods immediately.** Upon paying for the desired information, the customer can access it immediately. Shipping costs are non-existent.
- **No refunds.** Most businesses that sell information have a no-refund policy because, once delivered, the information cannot be "returned."

In order to successfully sell information on the Internet, the business must produce information that is in demand and of high quality. If you're thinking of selling articles, e-books, online courses or the like, realize that customers will expect you or your authors to be experts in the field. You should be able to back up claims of expertise with impressive experience or accomplishments.

Answer these questions to start thinking about information you could develop to sell online:

1. List industries or fields in which you have experience and how long you were involved in each. _____

   _____

   _____

2. What unique skills have you acquired as a result of your experience?

   _____

   _____

3. Have you developed any unique

   Methods to solve a problem? _____

   Materials to teach a skill? _____

   Steps to reach a goal? _____

   Strategies to motivate others? _____

   Tools to perform a task? _____

4. How will you package your information to sell online (e.g., articles, tutorials, e-books, etc.)? _____

   _____

For examples of Web sites that sell information, visit

- www.constant-content.com (Articles, tutorials, and product reviews)
- www.thearticlegroup.com (Ghost writers, article creation)
- www.forrester.com (Research results)
- www.hudforclosed.com (Homes in foreclosure)
- www.eplans.com (Construction plans)
- www.chiltondiy.com (Do-it-yourself automotive repair)

The information you provide should be free from errors and have an easy-to-read design and professional appearance. Digital information can be sold in formats other than the written word; e-businesses sell information using videos (DVDs, CDs, streaming video), podcasts, and audio files as well.

Give Customers a Taste

Businesses that sell information usually let customers view a small portion of the information for free to determine whether it is of adequate quality and relevant to their needs. Customers then pay a fee to purchase the remainder of the information.

Services for Sale: Service with a :-)

A wide variety of services are available through online businesses, including the following:

- Contractor referral
- Graphic design
- Web site design
- Charity registry
- Search engine optimization
- Web site hosting
- Online job search
- Classified advertising
- Wedding guide publisher
- Virtual secretary

- Travel agent
- Resume service
- Business plan consultant
- Document translation
- Debt collection
- Sales lead generators
- Editing and proofreading
- Internet research
- E-mail list management
- People searches

If you choose to start an online service business, you'll need to have some experience in that industry. Don't think that just because your business is delivered online (and people can't see you sitting at your computer in your pajamas) that you can enter a field where you have no expertise. You won't be a very good online travel agent if you don't understand how the travel industry works. You'll also have plenty of online (and offline) competition for your services, so you'll have to offer a compelling reason for customers to choose your business. As with any business start-up, choose a service business that is compatible with your expertise, skills, and interest.

Customers often choose a service business to perform tasks that they can't or won't do themselves. The customer who isn't (and doesn't want to become) computer savvy may hire an online Web site designer; the tax accountant who doesn't feel creative enough to write marketing copy for her firm's brochures may find an online copywriter. When deciding what online services you will offer, ask yourself what unique skills you have that are in high demand.

> Most online businesses have an "about us" section on their Web site outlining their years of experience, achievements, and recognizable clients.

Answer these questions as you think about a possible online service business:

1. List service industries where you have work experience. Can those services be delivered online? _____

   _____

   _____

2. How do you enjoy spending your time? Is there something you like to do that others don't? Can this be turned into a service that people will pay for? _____

   _____

   _____

3. What skills and experience do you have that others lack (financial, writing, translation, computer, etc.)? What do people say you do well? _____

_____

_____

If you launch an online service business, survey your customers frequently and ask for input concerning your Web site and your services. Consider what they tell you and make changes accordingly. Encourage repeat business and referrals by offering incentives, such as volume or referral discounts.

Setting Your E-business Apart from the Competition

While selling online provides an alternative way of doing business, the fundamental business principles remain the same: You must think of your business in terms of what need it fills or what problem it solves. The most successful online businesses sell products, information, or services that are in high demand, are unique, or fill a specific market niche. Consider the benefits your products or services provide to your potential customers. Finally, with those benefits in mind, create an online marketing strategy that will set your product apart from your competitors.

For example, let's say that your online business sells a unique backpack that can be worn like a traditional backpack but can also be rolled on built-in wheels and pulled with a telescoping handle.

- **Your target customer:** The nontraditional, older adult college student.
- **The problem your product solves:** The risk of shoulder and back pain or injury from transporting heavy textbooks in a conventional backpack.
- **The benefit your product provides:** A pain-free way to transport heavy textbooks over long distances.
- **Your marketing strategy:** Your Web site shows a video clip of an older adult student, smiling and walking at a brisk pace while rolling a backpack of books past much younger students who are grimacing and struggling with their heavy loads. Detailed photographs show the key features of your product up close. Back-to-school promotions offer 15% off during the months of July through September.

In the competitive Internet marketplace, your Web site must stand out from the competition. Unless your product or service is completely unique, you will need a creative marketing or customer service strategy that appeals to visitors. You could have online contests, offer free shipping, host a discussion board, send a monthly newsletter, or post daily affirmations. Get inspiration for your Web site by visiting these attention-grabbing sites:

- **Wide selection; free shipping:** Look at Zappos.com with its huge selection of inventory, multi-view options, and free shipping, even on returns (www.zappos.com).
- **Interesting online tools:** Eons.com, where the motto is "Loving life on the flip side of fifty," offers a life expectancy calculator plus tips on how to live longer (www.livingto100.com).

- **Distinctive or niche products:** Skeletons in the Closet is the Web site of the LA County coroner's gift shop that sells unusual gifts and apparel (www.lacoroner.com). Anything Left Handed sells products exclusively for left-handed people (www.anythingleft-handed.co.uk).
- **Creative use of technology:** Visit MediaSauce.com and see how this company uses Flash technology and podcasts in a unique and engaging way (www.mediasauce.com).

Be Passionate About Your Business

With all these options to choose from, how do you decide what type of online business is right for you? The bottom line is the same whether you are launching an e-business or a traditional bricks-and-mortar business: Start a business that is in line with your passion, experiences, skills, and values. Launching a new business venture is challenging, and if you don't have a passion for what you're doing—or worse yet, you dislike what you're doing—you won't feel successful, even if you achieve your financial goals.

Launching Your Web Site

While there are many options for getting the job done, the basic steps for launching a Web site are the same:

1. **Register a domain name.** Choose a name, check to see whether it's available, and register to use it.

2. **Build your Web site.** Design the layout and write the content of the pages of your site. If you plan to make sales from your Web site, you will need basic e-commerce tools:

   o A "Shopping Cart" that displays your items and lets customers click to buy.

   o A method of accepting credit card payments, either by opening your own merchant account or using a shopping cart service that allows you to use its merchant account.

3. **Host your Web site.** Choose a Web hosting company that allows your site to be seen online. Make sure that it allows for enough storage space and bandwidth (*bandwidth* regulates how many people can come visit your site within a given time period).

4. **Promote your Web site.** Employ strategies to drive traffic to your site.

Let's discuss some options for each of these steps.

Register a Domain Name

Before you can launch a Web site, you'll have to come up with a unique name for it. Web site names are called *domain names* and usually look like this: www.yourbusinessname.com. Domain names must be registered with Domain Name Registrars.

Your domain name should reflect your business and be easy to spell and remember. Finding a name that hasn't already been registered can be a challenge. Domain names must be at least two but no more than 63 characters long. They may include any combination of letters, numbers or hyphens, although the first and last character cannot be a hyphen. Names are not case sensitive, so www.WhiteHouse.gov is the same as www.whitehouse.gov. Start by making a list of possible names; consider using combinations of words, such as "iloveselfemployment."

Once you've made a list of possible domain names, check to see whether any of your choices are available. You can do this by visiting a registrar such as Verisign.com or NetworkSolutions.com. Many registrars allow you to search a list of possible domain names to find out which are still available.

When you register your domain name, expect to pay a yearly fee for your name. Most registrars sell single or multi-year contracts but no registrar is allowed to sell a contract for more than 10 years. The registrar should notify you before your contract expires, giving you an opportunity to renew your registration.

> Domain names consist of a name followed by a 'dot' and an extension. Familiar extensions include .com, .net, and .org, though others are available, such as .biz or .info. The name you want may not be available as a .com, the most common extension, but it may be available with a different extension. Just be aware that each of these extensions generally signifies something different (.com for business and .org for nonprofit organizations, for example).

Build Your Web Site

A professional-looking Web site makes a positive first impression on visitors. Business owners have many options for creating such a site. In this section we will look at three options for building your Web site: hiring a Web site designer, using a storefront builder, or purchasing and customizing a Web site template.

Hiring a Web Site Designer

Before hiring a Web designer, check out other sites the designer created and see if you like the quality and style of their work. Web sites should be easy to use, free of errors, and pleasing to look at. Ask the designer for a list of past clients you can call for references. Find out whether the designer was easy to work with, flexible, and dependable, and whether or not the finished product was worth the time and money.

Know what to expect from your designer: Will he or she write the content on your Web pages or will you be expected to provide it? Can your designer add the e-commerce aspects of your site, such as your shopping cart and a method for accepting online payments? Will the designers be available to maintain your site once it is launched, and if so, how much will you be charged for maintenance? Find out what, if any, services are provided to help you market your site once it is launched. Get a written contract or work order that spells out what the designer will and will not do and a timeframe in which the work will be performed. Work with the designer throughout the process, and review your pages as they are being developed.

Storefront Builders

A business owner on a limited budget with little or no technical skills might want to consider using a "storefront" service such as eBay ProStores. ProStores allow the user to build an online storefront complete with everything required to sell online. eBay's most basic service, ProStores Express, allows a user to sell up to 10 unique items on a two-page Web site for as little as $6.95 per month plus a small per-transaction fee.

ProStores offers easy-to-use design wizards and Web site templates that allow non-technical users to build a storefront quickly. They also offer secure online check-out for customers through PayPal, a payment processing service that allows customers to buy products online using credit, debit, and bank transfer payments. ProStores can be integrated into the eBay auction site as well, which could increase traffic to your storefront. More-expensive packages offer additional features such as unlimited pages, shipping integration, and report generators.

While eBay ProStores provides a quick and simple option for launching an eBusiness, it is not a perfect solution. One of the drawbacks to doing business through eBay is that most people who shop eBay are looking for a bargain. This means they are less likely to pay your prices if they can find lower prices on another eBay store or through the eBay auctions. While eBay brings many buyers together in one place, it attracts many sellers as well, which means that your competition will be stiff.

There are many other companies that offer storefront building as well as e-commerce solutions such as shopping carts and credit card processing. The following list includes some popular e-commerce companies and their Web site addresses.

E-commerce Solution	Web Site	Storefront Building	Shopping Cart	Credit Card Processing
eBay ProStores	www.prostores.com	X	X	X
GoEMerchant.com	www.goemerchant.com	X	X	X
Web.com	www.web.com	X	X	X
MonsterCommerce	www.monstercommerce.com	X	X	
StoreBuilderPlus	www.storebuilderplus.com	X	X	
Yahoo! Merchant Solutions	www.store.yahoo.com	X	X	
Volusions	www.volusion.com	X	X	

Purchase a Template

Another option for designing a Web site is to purchase a professional template. Templates are typically sold with one or two designs for the home page and a few alternative designs for the other (content) pages of your site. They are typically designed by professional graphic artists and have a high-quality appearance. Once you purchase and download your template, you will be able to customize and edit it using graphics software such as Adobe Photoshop and Web site development software such as Macromedia Dreamweaver.

Templates provide a simple way to create a professional-looking Web site without having to learn to write complicated "code." While free template software is available on the Internet, the more sophisticated and professional templates are well worth the $50–$150 investment. If you are willing to pay for it, most template companies will also customize your template for you. Don't forget to add the e-commerce features such as a shopping cart and a way to accept payments online.

Regardless of the method you choose to build your Web site, the next step is to find a Web hosting company to make your site available to customers.

Host Your Web Site

Web hosting companies have computers (called *servers*) that are connected to the Internet. Once you've opened an account with a Web host, you can send or upload your Web site files. The Web host places *(publishes)* your files into space you rent on its server. Once your site is published, it can be viewed by anyone through the Internet.

Many Web hosting companies offer a variety of services in addition to hosting, including domain name registration, free Web site templates, and easy-to-use Web site development software and e-commerce services. They usually provide e-mail accounts that include your domain name and programs designed to drive traffic to your Web site. For this reason, you might want to compare Web hosting companies early in the process of building your e-business.

Hosting companies typically charge a monthly fee for their services; some charge as little as $3.00 per month for basic hosting services. Additional services cost extra. To the right are names and Web site addresses of some popular hosting companies.

Hosting Company	Web Address
Yahoo!	smallbusiness.yahoo.com
GoDaddy	www.godaddy.com
Dotster	www.dotster.com
Network Solutions	www.networksolutions.com
HostGator	www.hostgator.com
HostMonster	www.hostmonster.com
StartLogic	www.startlogic.com
Aplus	www.aplus.net
Dot5	www.dot5hosting.com
HostRocket	www.hostrocket.com
BlueHost	www.bluehost.com

Promote Your Web Site

It is impossible to know how many Web sites are on the Internet—the number changes by the minute. In February 2007, the Netcraft Web Server Survey found more than 108 million distinct Web sites consisting of an estimated 30 billion pages. Getting people to visit your Web site won't just happen; it will take some work on your part to drive traffic to your site.

There are two distinct ways to market your Web site: offline and online. Offline refers to all the traditional marketing strategies you can use to promote your site, such as these:

- Include your Web site address on all printed materials related to your business, such as stationery, business cards, yellow page ads, flyers, and brochures.
- Include your Web site information in all display or classified ads you purchase.
- Write articles for trade or professional journals and include your Web site address in your contact information.
- Don't forget about word of mouth. Mention your Web site address often.

You can also market your Web site online. One way to do this is to rank high in search engines. Search engines (SEs) are software that search the Internet for information entered by a user and return a list of Web sites that contain that information. Some common SEs are Google, Yahoo!, MSN, and Ask.com. The higher a Web site is ranked by an SE, the closer to the top of the list it appears and the greater the chance that that site will be visited by a user.

Before an SE can rank your site, it has to find it. One way to be found is to submit your Web site to the SEs and directories. Some search engines accept free submissions of commercial Web sites but others may charge an annual fee. Unfortunately, submitting your site to a search engine does not guarantee it will be listed. SE submission and SE optimization—altering your site so that it ranks well—are complex processes. To learn more, visit Web sites such as www.searchenginewatch.com or www.seologic.com.

Other ways to market your Web site include the following:

- Get related Web sites to include a link to your site.
- Create an e-newsletter that site visitors can sign up for. Encourage them to pass it along to others.
- Include useful resources on your site and update them often.
- Add a free tool on your site to attract visitors.

Planning Your E-business

Use the following worksheet to begin planning your e-business. Keep in mind that this represents the preliminary stages of starting your business and that you will still need to follow most, if not all, of the other steps outlined in this book. For example, you may still need to raise capital, price your products or services, and manage your cash flow. And of course you should still create a business plan. An e-business requires all the same forethought, energy, and careful management of any other business.

My Web Site Planning Worksheet

Purpose of my Web site (check all that apply):

❑ Inform potential clients about my business

❑ Sell products, services, or information online

❑ Publish my prices online

❑ Market my bricks-and-mortar business

❑ Market my online business

❑ Promote sales items and specials

❑ Provide customers with useful links and other resources

❑ Other: _____

My Web site vision (why I want a Web site and what I hope to accomplish):

_____

_____

_____

Information (content) on my Web site will include (check all that apply):

❑ Company history/About us page

❑ Staff directory/biographical information

❑ Products for sale (❑ online   ❑ at a bricks-and-mortar location   ❑ both)

❑ Services for sale (❑ online   ❑ at a bricks-and-mortar location   ❑ both)

❑ Information for sale (❑ online   ❑ at a bricks-and-mortar location   ❑ both)

❑ A regular newsletter feature

❑ Contact information (address, phone number, e-mail address, fax number, physical location)

❑ A blog or discussion page

❑ List of existing clients/referrals

❑ Customer service information

❑ E-mail account(s)

❑ Refund policies

❑ Privacy policies

❑ Access to online purchases (shopping cart/credit card processing)

❑ Resource page (suggested reading, Web site links, etc.)

❑ Other: _____

❑ Other: _____

❑ Other: _____

(continued)

(continued)

Web Site Planning and Costs

Domain name

My domain name is: _____

I will register my domain name through _____ at a cost of $_____ per _____

Web site building

❑ I will hire a Web site designer at a cost of $_____

❑ I will purchase a storefront package at a cost of $ _____ per _____

❑ I will purchase a template from _____ at a cost of $_____

❑ I will need the following software to edit my template:

_____ $ _____

_____ $ _____

❑ My e-commerce services will be purchased from _____

and will include_____ at a cost of $ _____

Hosting

My Web site hosting company will be _____

at a cost of $_____ per _____

Schedule

I plan to have my Web site design completed by: _____

I plan to have my Web site published by: _____

Marketing

My offline marketing will include: _____

_____

_____

My online marketing will include: _____

_____

_____

Glossary of E-commerce Terms

The following are terms you should be familiar with before starting an online business:

Affiliate program: An automated marketing system that allows companies to generate leads and sales from other Web sites. An advertising company creates an online ad with a link back to its site. A Web site agrees to "host" the ad (place the ad on its Web site). Visitors to the hosting Web site click on the ad and are directed to the advertiser's Web site. If the visitor makes a purchase from the advertiser, the host Web site receives a fee.

Banner ad: An online advertisement intended to attract traffic to a Web site. When a viewer clicks on a banner ad, the viewer is directed to the advertiser's Web site.

Blog: An online journal intended to reflect the views of its creator. Blogs are frequently updated and intended for public viewing. The creator of a blog is a "blogger"; updating a blog is called "blogging." Small businesses can use blogs to entice customers to visit frequently (provided the business's blogs are intriguing or informative).

Browser: The software that provides an easy-to-use interface for accessing the World Wide Web. Browsers allow users to "surf" the Internet and view Web pages. Common browsers include Microsoft's Internet Explorer and Netscape Navigator.

Click through: The process of clicking through an online advertisement to the advertiser's Web site. The click through rate (CTR), defined as a percent, is the number of clicks on an ad divided by the number of times the ad was displayed.

Cookie: Information stored on a user's computer by Web sites the user has visited. Cookies contain information that the Web site uses to track visits. The only personal information a cookie can contain is information supplied by the user, such as a user name or contact information. Other information may include which Web site pages were visited and user preferences. E-businesses use cookies to automatically log-in repeat customers or customize Web pages based on previous visits.

Domain name: A unique name that identifies a Web site, such as www.mydomain.com.

Search engine: Software that searches the Internet for information entered by the user, and returns a list of Web sites that contain that information. Examples of search engines are Google, Yahoo!, and Lycos.

Search engine optimization: The process of designing a Web site's content so that it ranks highly in various search engines. The higher a Web site ranks by a search engine, the greater the chance that that site will be visited by a user.

SSL or Secure Sockets Layer Certificate: An SSL certificate gives a Web site the ability to communicate securely with its Web customers. It identifies the merchant using it and is used to encrypt credit card information and other sensitive data. A must-have for anyone selling over the Internet.

Server: A computer that stores and delivers or "serves" up information to other computers that are linked through a network.

Web host: Web hosts use their servers to store Web files, typically for a fee. The server then allows Web sites to be accessed and viewed over the Internet.

Summing Up

There is no question that e-business is growing and that every day entrepreneurs are using technology to start businesses from their desks at home. The notion that e-business owners can launch a Web site and then wait for the money to roll in is pure fantasy, however. With more than a billion Internet users searching some 30 billion pages of data, the competition to draw traffic to your site is great. Having a successful e-business takes work. Time and effort must go into building and launching a site, and promoting that site is an ongoing challenge. But with its low start-up costs, an e-business can be quite rewarding for the entrepreneur willing to do the research and the hard work required to make it successful.

Business Plan

Cathy's Cleaning Service, Inc.

Cathy Smith, President
P.O. Box 0000
Anytown, IN 40000
(317) 000-0000
Cathy@ccsi-anytown.com
www.ccsi-anytown.com

Cathy's Cleaning Service, Inc.
Business Plan

Introduction

Description of Business

Cathy's Cleaning Service, Inc. (CCSI), is a full-service residential and commercial cleaning company. The business has been owned and operated by Cathy Smith since June 2XXX and is a Sub-S corporation, incorporated in June 2XXX. The business is operated out of Cathy Smith's home office. The mailing address is P.O. Box 0000, Anytown, IN, 40000. The business phone number is (317) 000-0000.

In June 2XXX, Cathy Smith was a mother of two school-age children and a full-time homemaker when she began cleaning homes for neighbors. Within six months, Cathy was regularly cleaning two residences and had one commercial property contract. She hired her mother and two sisters as part-time employees and has since added to her staff.

Currently, CCSI has three full-time and four part-time employees who work in teams to provide services to clients. Two of the full-time employees and three of the part-time employees make up the commercial cleaning department, and the remaining employees operate in the residential cleaning department.

Commercial contracts are awarded annually, and residential cleaning is done on an ongoing basis unless a homeowner wishes to make a change.

The business goal of CCSI is to provide high-quality residential and commercial cleaning services to customers at a reasonable price that will allow the corporation and its owner to recognize a profit. It is also the mission of the company to foster a healthy working environment, to pay competitive and fair wages to its employees, and to encourage employees to develop a healthy balance between work and family commitments.

The company owner recently completed a business planning course to improve her ability to analyze and monitor pricing and produce long- and short-term cash-flow projections. Additionally, the owner and one manager intend to complete a personnel management course by the end of the year. A short-term capital equipment loan is required to add industrial vacuums and other cleaning equipment, thereby allowing the firm to grow by taking on more commercial contracts.

Marketing

Service Description

CCSI offers residential and light commercial cleaning. For residential customers, each job is bid according to the size of the home, the number of individuals residing in the home, and the scope of services required. The homeowner can choose from three service packages. These are outlined below:

- Residential Cleaning #1—Frequency of visits: 1–4 times per month. Includes dusting of all surfaces, vacuuming all carpeted areas, sweeping and mopping all vinyl or tile floor areas, complete bathroom cleaning, loading dirty dishes into a dishwasher (no hand washing dishes), up to three full loads of laundry (washed, dried, folded, and stacked), general light housecleaning.

- Residential Cleaning #2—Frequency of visits: 1–4 times per month. Includes dusting of all surfaces, vacuuming all carpeted areas, sweeping and mopping all vinyl or tile floor areas, complete bathroom cleaning, general light housecleaning.

- Residential Cleaning #3—Frequency of visits: One-time cleaning. Includes all of the services offered in package #1, plus window washing (inside only) and oven cleaning. This cost of this package is an actual per-hour cost of $20.00 per hour per cleaning person.

The most commonly purchased residential package is #1. Package #2 is usually ordered by the single customer or the customer who may not work full time outside of the home. Package #3 is most often ordered for special occasions, such as weddings or family reunions. Custom packages are available for customers who have special needs.

Commercial cleaning is bid on a custom basis. The owners or property managers of a commercial building will meet with the owner of CCSI and decide on the frequency of visits and services to be offered. Commonly, the services performed in commercial buildings include emptying trash and ash receptacles, vacuuming carpeted areas, damp mopping vinyl and tile floor areas, and cleaning rest rooms. The professional cleaners of CCSI will not remove or disturb anything atop desks or other personal work areas. Work surfaces, computers, and other electronic equipment will be lightly dusted but not disturbed. All bids for services are prepared by Cathy Smith.

Market Description

CCSI is located on the near East side of Anytown. The target markets for cleaning services are the residential and commercial customers located on the East and near East sides of Anytown.

The primary residential target customers are families who have both parents working outside the home and who have two or more children. According to *American Demographic* magazine, 43 percent of families of four or larger in which both parents are employed outside the home utilize a professional housecleaning service at least once a month. Of that 43 percent, 51 percent prefer to use a local, privately owned service as opposed to a franchise operation. They state that the reasons for this preference are more dependable service, greater ability to customize services, and more flexible working agreements.

The second target market for residential customers is the single executive. *American Demographic* magazine finds that 37 percent of singles earning an annual income of $40,000 or greater utilize a cleaning service at least once a month.

According to the 2XXX census report for Anytown, 22 percent of all metropolitan Anytown families of four or larger in which both parents are working outside the home live in the near East side and the East side neighborhoods of Anytown. Only 7 percent of the single executives earning annual incomes of $40,000 or greater reside in this same geographic area.

The commercial market CCSI targets is small office buildings that employ 50 or fewer employees. Larger offices tend to utilize large, franchise cleaning services, and very large, multi-business office buildings often have on-staff cleaning services. Industrial buildings are often quite difficult and time-consuming to clean and are not included in the target market for CCSI.

According to the *Commercial Real Estate Update* (local) magazine, the near East side of Anytown contains more than 30 percent of all small commercial office buildings in the downtown or near downtown areas.

Competition

As of December 31, 2XXX, only two privately owned cleaning services and no franchise services specifically serviced this geographic area of Anytown. Comparatively, 27 privately owned services and four large franchise services target the North, Northwest, and Northeast areas of metropolitan Anytown. The South, Southeast, and Southwest areas are serviced by another 15 companies, and the West side of town is targeted by another 12 companies. Even though the East and near East side neighborhoods do not make up the largest portion of the target residential customer, the lack of existing competition and the existing contacts CCSI has established make this a very good market in which to sell its services. The facts that CCSI has an office located on the near East side and that all of its employees live on the East side allow CCSI to be more responsive to customer needs.

Cathy's Cleaning Service _____ Business Plan Pg. 3

Most commercial cleaning services prefer to bid on the larger multi-office office buildings, and a survey conducted by CCSI and mailed to local office buildings found that the smaller buildings have had difficulty finding services willing to clean their offices.

Direct Competition

CCSI has two direct competitors on the near East side: Custom Cleaners and Quick Cleaning Service. Both competitors are privately owned. Customer Cleaners consists of one employee, the business owner, Marge Maple. Ms. Maple is a mother of two who cleans part-time, three days per week, while her children are in school. She cleans for a few long-time residential customers but does no commercial cleaning. She is not licensed or bonded and at this time is not accepting new clients.

Quick Cleaning Service is locally owned and has a staff of 6 to 8 full- and part-time employees. Its employees are licensed and bonded. Quick Cleaning offers both residential and commercial cleaning services to customers on the near East side. Its training program teaches employees to clean residential properties using only bottled cleaning solutions and cotton hand towels that are reused throughout the job. They are trained not to use water for any cleaning other than mopping floors. The cleaning quality of this approach is less than desireable. They also use the customers' residential-quality vacuum cleaners to vacuum floors.

As part of competition research, Quick Cleaning Service was hired to clean the home of Cathy Smith's mother. The quality of the cleaning was quite poor; kitchen and bathroom counter tops were streaked and dirt remained in crevices; cobwebs were not cleaned from the ceilings and air vents; the basboards were not wiped clean; some furniture pieces were not dusted; and the home had an overpowering smell as a result of air freshners that the cleaning service used.

Quick Cleaning Service's residential rates are 10% higher than CCSI's. Its commercial rates are comparable but employees perform fewer services for commerical clients; for example, they do not damp mop vinyl and tile floors. In the past 12 months, it has lost at least two commercial clients due to poor performace.

Competition Summary

CCSI offers service to an area that is poorly serviced at this time. CCSI also offers custom cleaning services tailored to the specific size of each location and the services requested by the individual customer—something the larger franchise firms do not offer. For residential and commercial customers alike, the fact that CCSI has established a reputation for honest, dependable cleaning people is quite attractive. All employees are bonded, and a police background check is performed prior to hire to ensure high-quality employees. Supervisors are assigned to monitor work crews, thereby providing added security for the customer.

Marketing Strategy

CCSI markets its cleaning services through advertisements in the local *Near Eastside Neighbor* and *Anytown East* newspapers. Additionally, five local church bulletins are used to advertise services. Fliers are posted at four local beauty shops, one local grocery store, and two service stations. A referral program is being offered to existing customers whereby an existing customer who refers a new customer gets a $25 discount on future cleaning services.

Through a local property management company, which manages 70 single-family rental units, one free housecleaning will be awarded (program to begin next month) to a resident who wins this service in a semiannual drawing (all residents who pay their rent early or on time for six months in a row are eligible for the drawing). In the commercial buildings CCSI cleans, one free residential cleaning will be awarded per year to each customer to be given away as the commercial building owner/manager wishes (such as to employees as an "employee of the year" award). Also, cleaning gift certificates for $25, $50, $75, and $100 will be offered to commercial accounts as gifts for employees or preferred customers. Of course, these gift certificates will also be available to residential customers. Once every quarter, all residential and commercial customers will receive a newsletter outlining all current marketing programs.

Word-of-mouth advertising still remains the most effective method of growth for CCSI. All customer suggestions are responded to in writing, and all phone calls are returned within 24 hours. By paying special attention to all customers and frequently (at least once a quarter) contacting all customers by telephone or in person to see whether they remain satisfied with the level of services offered, CCSI continues to build a loyal clientele.

Pricing Strategy

While all jobs are bid based on estimated cleaning time plus materials, the average residential customer is charged $90 per cleaning and cleaning is done twice a month.

Commercial accounts are also estimated based on size and scope of the job. An average commercial account is charged $125 per week and is cleaned 4.3 weeks per month.

Organization

Quality Control

CCSI recognizes the importance of delivering high-quality service in order to maintain a loyal customer base. To ensure that cleaning is done to the high standards of CCSI, supervisors regularly inspect the work performed. For residential customers who contract CCSI to clean regularly, at least one cleaning per month is supervised by a manager. For residential customers who contract a single or special-event cleaning, every work crew is headed by a manager who supervises the cleaning. Every commercial work crew is accompanied by a manager who supervises the cleaning of office buildings.

Work crews are scheduled weekly. Two full-time and three part-time employees are regularly scheduled to perform on the commercial contracts. One full-time and one part-time employee regularly clean residential properties. Cathy Smith regularly accompanies work crews as a supervisor. Each work crew has a checklist that must be reviewed before leaving the work site. The checklist ensures that all services contracted are actually performed. The crew leader signs the checklist and becomes responsible for any discrepancies reported by the customer. All cleaning products are provided by CCSI unless a customer specifically requests that a certain product be used. This ensures consistent use of high-quality cleaning products.

CCSI's quarterly contact with every customer allows customers to voice any concerns or complaints they may have regarding the quality of work performed. Customer suggestions are always considered and implemented whenever possible.

Legal Structure

CCSI is a Sub-S corporation, incorporated in June 2XXX. The business is operated by the sole owner, Cathy Smith. CCSI originally started doing business in 2XXX as a sole proprietorship and converted to a Sub-S for limited liability protection and tax purposes.

Insurance

CCSI carries business liability insurance through Mr. Allen Green of the ABC Insurance Agency. The insurance underwriter is AmerInsurance.

Additionally, all employees of CCSI are bonded. Workers' Compensation and a life insurance policy on Cathy Smith are also sold to CCSI by the same agency.

Management

Cathy Smith is the President and General Manager of CCSI. Her background includes supervisory positions for more than 10 years, managing as many as 15 employees in a manufacturing environment. Cathy left the job market for 10 years when she married and had two children, and she began CCSI when her youngest child started first grade.

Cathy's Cleaning Service _____ Business Plan Pg. 6

Cathy hires and trains employees, schedules residential and commercial cleaning, purchases supplies, negotiates contracts, and markets the company. Each cleaning crew has a crew leader who immediately supervises all work, and each division has a manager who takes responsibility for supervising the crew leaders. Additionally, Cathy acts as a manager in both divisions.

The manager in the commercial cleaning division, Sarah Jones, has five years of experience working as a manager for a national franchise cleaning service. Sarah has worked for CCSI since October 2XXX.

The residential cleaning division manager, Mary Murphy, has two years of experience as the head of housekeeping services for a large local hotel. Mary has been employed with CCSI since January 2XXX.

Cathy maintains accounts receivable and payable for CCSI. She collects all business-related receipts and maintains the company checkbook and other records. On a quarterly schedule, Cathy turns these records over to a bookkeeper, who prepares quarterly profit and loss statements. Once a year, a Certified Public Accountant prepares the company taxes and generates a full set of financial statements.

Actual payroll generation and payroll tax records are maintained by PAYCHECKS, Inc., a payroll service. Payroll is generated on the fifteenth and last day of each month.

Advisors

James Smith, CPA, prepares taxes and annual financial statements for CCSI. Mr. Smith, Cathy's husband, is in private practice with an office located at 123 Main Street, Anytown. Jane Kennedy, a local attorney with Mayor, Jones, and Smith, is CCSI's attorney. Mr. Smith and Ms. Kennedy advised CCSI to convert to a Sub-S corporation and Ms. Kennedy filed all the appropriate paperwork with the Secretary of State. Annually, Cathy meets with both Mr. Smith and Ms. Kennedy to review the status of the company and to discuss any updates or changes that need to be made.

Cathy has also compiled a group of four volunteers who serve as an advisory committee. Once a year, Cathy meets with these advisors to discuss her business strategies and update her business plan. Three of the four advisors are retired executives who offer their expertise based on many years of small business experience. The fourth advisor is a local businesswoman who manages a financial services business. Two of her four advisors are also CCSI customers.

Cathy's Cleaning Service _____ Business Plan Pg. 7

Financial Information

Use of Funds

Use of loan proceeds will be as follows:

Loan Request: $5,000.00

Use of funds is for permanent working capital. A cash-flow projection, which demonstrates that this influx of cash will allow CCSI to service more residential and commercial customers, follows. The projection outlines that the increase in sales will allow CCSI to purchase additional capital equipment beginning in the first month. The cash-flow projections also demonstrate an adequate ability to service the debt incurred by this loan.

The proposed loan will be secured with a first security interest in the assets of the business, as well as a personal guaranty from Cathy Smith. CCSI has no business debt at this time and owns equipment with a net value (net of accumulated depreciation) of $3,500.00 and intends to purchase new equipment valued at $1,900.

Cash-Flow Assumptions

The first assumption of the cash-flow projection is that all existing business will be retained in the next 12 months. New residential business will be in the form of two new houses cleaned twice a month in month 2, a third new house in month 4, a fourth new house in month 6, and a minor increase in rates in month 10 for a total new residential business income of $7,080.

New commercial business consists of one new building in month 3, a second new building in month 5, and a slight increase in all commercial rates reflected in months 9–12. Total new commercial income for the year is $10,176.

The operating expenses related to existing business will remain 40 percent of income. The operating expenses related to new business income are reflected as 38 percent of new residential income and 38 percent of new commercial income.

This assumption is based on historical operating percentages. All fixed expenses remain the same. Since this business is operated from Cathy's home office, there are no rent or utility expenses. Loan payments begin in month 2 and are calculated on borrowing $5,000 at 10 percent interest for a 36-month term.

Capital equipment purchases will include three new vacuum cleaners in months 1, 3, and 5, and a floor waxing unit in month 7.

Cathy's Cleaning Service_____ Business Plan Pg. 8

Cathy's Cleaning Service, Inc.

12-Month Cash-Flow Forecast	1	2	3	4	5	6
Beginning Cash Balance	$850	$5,045	$4,396	$3,631	$3,428	$3,107
Cash Inflow						
Existing Business	$3,200	$3,200	$3,200	$3,200	$3,200	$3,200
Loan Proceeds	$5,000					
Owner Contributions						
New Residential Business		$360	$360	$540	$540	$720
New Commercial Business			$538	$538	$1,075	$1,075
Total Cash Inflow	$8,200	$3,560	$4,098	$4,278	$4,815	$4,995
Cash Outflow						
Existing Operating Expenses	$1,280	$1,280	$1,280	$1,280	$1,280	$1,280
New Residential Operating Exp	$0	$137	$137	$205	$205	$274
New Commercial Operating Exp	$0	$0	$204	$204	$409	$409
Office Supplies	$35	$35	$35	$35	$35	$35
Business Insurance	$30	$30	$30	$30	$30	$30
Auto Expense	$120	$120	$120	$120	$120	$120
Auto Insurance	$35	$35	$35	$35	$35	$35
Business Cell Phone	$55	$55	$55	$55	$55	$55
Loan Payments		$517	$517	$517	$517	$517
Owner's Compensation	$2,000	$2,000	$2,000	$2,000	$2,000	$2,000
Capital Purchase—Vacuum Clnrs	$450		$450		$450	
Capital Purchase—Floor Waxer						
Total Cash Outflow	$4,005	$4,209	$4,863	$4,481	$5,136	$4,755
Monthly Change in Cash	$4,195	($649)	($765)	($203)	($321)	$240
Ending Cash Balance	$5,045	$4,396	$3,631	$3,428	$3,107	$3,347

Cathy's Cleaning Service _____ Business Plan Pg. 9

Cathy's Cleaning Service, Inc.

12-Month Cash-Flow Forecast	7	8	9	10	11	12	Totals
Beginning Cash Balance	$3,347	$3,037	$3,277	$3,595	$3,963	$4,331	
Cash Inflow							
Existing Business	$3,200	$3,200	$3,200	$3,200	$3,200	$3,200	$38,400
Loan Proceeds							$5,000
Owner Contributions							$0
New Residential Business	$720	$720	$720	$800	$800	$800	$7,080
New Commercial Business	$1,075	$1,075	$1,200	$1,200	$1,200	$1,200	$10,176
Total Cash Inflow	$4,995	$4,995	$5,120	$5,200	$5,200	$5,200	$60,656
Cash Outflow							
Existing Operating Expenses	$1,280	$1,280	$1,280	$1,280	$1,280	$1,280	$15,360
New Residential Operating Expenses	$274	$274	$274	$304	$304	$304	$2,690
New Commercial Operating Expenses	$409	$409	$456	$456	$456	$456	$3,867
Office Supplies	$35	$35	$35	$35	$35	$35	$420
Business Insurance	$30	$30	$30	$30	$30	$30	$360
Auto Expense	$120	$120	$120	$120	$120	$120	$1,440
Auto Insurance	$35	$35	$35	$35	$35	$35	$420
Business Cell Phone	$55	$55	$55	$55	$55	$55	$660
Loan Payments	$517	$517	$517	$517	$517	$517	$5,687
Owner's Compensation	$2,000	$2,000	$2,000	$2,000	$2,000	$2,000	$24,000
Capital Purchase—Vacuum Clnrs							$1,350
Capital Purchase—Floor Waxer	$550						$550
Total Cash Outflow	$5,305	$4,755	$4,802	$4,832	$4,832	$4,832	$56,806
Monthly Change in Cash	($310)	$240	$318	$368	$368	$368	$3,849
Ending Cash Balance	$3,037	$3,277	$3,595	$3,963	$4,331	$4,699	$4,699

Cathy's Cleaning Service _____ Business Plan Pg. 10

Recommended Resources

Books

Brabec, B. *Homemade Money: How to Select, Start, Manage, Market and Multiply the Profits of a Business At Home.* Cincinnati: Betterway, 1997.

Cook, M. *Home Business, Big Business: The Definitive Guide to Starting and Operating On-Line and Traditional Home-Based Ventures.* New York: Macmillan, 1998.

Covey, S. *Principle-Centered Leadership.* New York: Simon & Schuster, 1992.

Covey, S. *The Seven Habits of Highly Effective People.* New York: Simon & Schuster, 1990.

Edwards, P., & S. Edwards and L. Clampitt-Douglas. *Getting Business to Come to You: A Complete Do-It-Yourself Guide to Attracting All the Business You Can Enjoy.* New York: Penguin Putnam, Inc., 1998.

Edwards, P., & S. Edwards and L. Rohrbough. *Making Money in Cyberspace.* New York: J.P. Tarcher/Putnam, 1998

Fox, S. *Internet Riches: The Simple Money-Making Secrets of Online Millionaires.* New York: AMACOM, 2006.

Kem, C., and T. Hoffman Wolfgram. *Run Your Own Home Business (Here's How).* New York: McGraw-Hill, 1998.

Levinson, J. *Guerrilla Marketing: Secrets for Making Profits from Your Small Business.* New York: Houghton Mifflin, 1998.

McAleese, T. *Money: How to Get It, Keep It, and Make It Grow.* Broomall: Chelsea House, 1997.

McKain, S. *All Business Is Show Business: Strategies for Earning Standing Ovations from Your Customers.* Nashville: Rutledge Hill Press, 2002.

Ries, A., & J. Trout. *Marketing Warfare.* New York: McGraw-Hill, 1997.

Russel, C.L. *eBay Income: How Anyone of Any Age, Location, and/or Background Can Build a Highly Profitable Online Business with eBay.* Ocala: Atlantic Publishing Group, 2006.

Stansell, K. *Bootstrapper's Success Secrets: 151 Tactics for Building Your Business on a Shoestring Budget.* Franklin Lakes: Career Press, 1997.

Stolze, W. *Start Up: An Entrepreneur's Guide to Launching and Managing a New Business.* Franklin Lakes: Career Press, 1999.

Web Sites

www.entrepreneur.com—Includes feature articles and columns from *Entrepreneur Magazine*.

www.entreworld.org—An online resource for small business owners, the EntreWorld search engine delivers useful information, guidance, and contacts for the entrepreneur.

www.inc.com—This magazine and corresponding Web site on entrepreneurship provide hands-on advice, case studies, and overviews on the state of small business in the U.S.

www.irs.gov—The Internal Revenue Service Web site offers helpful tax information for small businesses as well as individuals.

www.quickbooks.intuit.com—QuickBooks Web site offers information about QuickBooks accounting software for specific industries.

www.sba.gov—Find resources and a FAQ from the Small Business Administration on starting up a small business.

www.smallbizhelp.net—A help center for small or home-based business owners, anyone who wants to start a small or home-based business, entrepreneurs, independent publishers, and mail-order dealers. This site offers marketing newsletters, below-wholesale product sources, success books, Internet marketing resources, home-based business opportunities, and more.

www.businesstown.com—This small-business site contains hundreds of key links, plus information on topics such as firing employees, selling your business, marketing, and doing taxes.

Index

F

failure, 5–6
financial plans, 24–26
   exercise, 25–26
Financial Statement worksheet, 131–132
financial statements, 121–134
   assets, 124, 130
   balance sheets, 121–122, 125, 127
   cash-flow statements, 121
   charts of accounts, 129
   credit transactions, 128–129
   equity, 124–126, 130
   exercise, 123
   expenses, 130
   Financial Statement worksheet, 131–132
   income statements, 121–122, 127, 130
   liabilities, 124, 130
   net worth, 125
   owner's equity, 125
   projections, 121
   questions, 133
   reasons for, 122
   retained earnings, 125–126, 130
financing, 19–31
   current situation, 19
   debt, 21
   existing businesses, 21–22
   financial plan exercise, 25–26
   free money, 22
   loan application process, 27
   loans, 23–31
   needs, identifying, 23–24
   new business, 21
   risks, 21
   Small Business Administration, 22
   terminology, 20–21
Five Cs of lending, 27
fixed expenses, 45
Fixed Expenses worksheet, 52–53
forrester.com Web site, 139
Four Ps of finance, 28
free money, 22

G

general partnerships, 90–91
   advantages, 91
   disadvantages, 91
   forming, 91
   tax issues, 91
gifts, personal, 11
goals
   action plan exercise, 40
   action plans, 36–37, 40

   personal, 12
   Practice Writing Effective Goals worksheet,
     35–36
   scenarios, evaluating, 38–39
   setting, 33–36
GoDaddy Web site, 145
GoEMerchant.com Web site, 144
government, market research, 65–66
grants, 23
gross income, defined, 45
gross profit, defined, 45

H

HostGator Web site, 145
hosting Web sites, 145
HostMonster Web site, 145
HostRocket Web site, 145
hudforclosed.com Web site, 139

I

ideas, business, 11–13
inc.com Web site, 164
income statements, 121–122, 127, 130
indirect competition, 71–72
independent contractors, 119
inexperience, 6
information-based products, 138–139
insurance, 97–101
   choosing, 99–100
   planning, 99
   priorities, 101
   types, 98
interest, loans, 30–31
Internet, market research, 65
invoices, defined, 104
IRS
   publications, 118
   Web site, 164

J–K

Journaling Activity worksheet, 114–116
journals, 109–111; *see also* cash receipt and disbursement journals
journals/periodicals, market research, 65
knowledge, customer, 6
knowledge-based goods, 138

L

LA County coroner's Web site, 142
launching Web sites, 142–146
legal forms of business, 6, 89–101
   choosing, 95–97
   corporations, 92–95